Jerusalem Through The Windows Of Time

Abraham Stahl

The Joint Authority for Jewish Zionist Education
The Department for Torah Education & Culture in the Diaspora
The Department for Jewish Education & Culture in the Diaspora
The Youth and Hechalutz Department
The Pedagogic Center

Sponsored by The Joint Program for Jewish Education of the Jewish Agency for Israel,
The World Zionist Organization, and the State of Israel, Ministry of Education and Culture

Producer and Coordinator: Nechama Cohn

Pedagogic Advisor: Dr. Dov Goldflam

Steering Committee:
Haim Weinreb
Rafi Banai
Arden Geldman
Hayim Azses

Consultants: Dr. G.H. Cohn, Jewish Sources
              Hagai Segev, Archaeology

Research: Shira Carmon

Translation: Chaim Mayerson
English Editor: Gila Ansell Brauner

Graphic Design: Studio Shmulik/ Yifat Gurion
68, Habanim st. Hod Hasharon 45268

ISBN : 965-403-103-5
Printed in Israel

Production and Marketing by

RECHES
Publishing House,
Educational Projects Ltd.,
P.O. Box 75, Even Yehuda 40550, Israel

P R E F A C E

Jerusalem, which encompasses within it the very essence of the Jewish people's past, the infinite facets of its existence - and its future -, is celebrating 3,000 years since King David decreed it his capital. From then to the present day, all the motifs of our history have been interwoven into the fabric of the city - redemption, persecution, expulsion, schism and unity, peace and fraternity. Both a spiritual and a national center, Jerusalem is the ultimate symbol of the Jewish people.

The marking of Jerusalem's trimillenial anniversary, therefore, denotes more than a "birthday" celebration for one of the most ancient cities in the history of the entire world: it is a festival marking our existence as a people, recognizing our culture, our spiritual achievements and our nationhood.

The Joint Authority for Jewish Zionist Education has decided to declare *Jerusalem* the theme for the school year of 5756 (1995-1996). Our goal is to focus all educational activity in Jewish centers worldwide on those concepts which have been central to our people throughout the ages.

The inherent educational potential is immense: the educator can develop the topic in any of the numerous and varied directions to which it lends itself, in order to generate his or her students' interest in our people's history and its continuity.

"Jerusalem Through the Windows of Time" tells the story of twelve major periods in the Jewish history of Jerusalem in pictures and in the words of Sages and saints, archaeologists and architects, story tellers and poets, historians and heroes.

It is our sincere hope that this book will become the backbone of Jerusalem programming throughout the year, in the hands of both educators and students alike. It is the outcome of work by a professional team in Jerusalem, which collaborated in close and constant consultation with specialists in many countries - testimony, perhaps, to the centrality of Jerusalem to all.

During the course of this year, there will be a great variety of special events to mark its importance. Our eyes will be turned to those which hold, undoubtedly, the greatest degree of importance: the programs organized by agencies and centers of Jewish education in the communities of Israel everywhere. For are we not commanded to "tell of them and repeat them" to our children, the key to future and continuing chapters of our people's existence?

Dr. David Harman,
Director General,
The Joint Authority for
Jewish Zionist Education

Table of Contents

JERUSALEM TODAY -
CENTER OF PEOPLE
AND COUNTRY

Jerusalem today - an aerial view

Jerusalem Today - Center of People and Country

Jerusalem has been the center of Jewish existence ever since the city was captured by King David some three thousand years ago. Even when the vast majority of Jews lived in exile, yearning for Jerusalem remained a central feature of Jewish life. Through the entire history of Jerusalem, there was hardly a time when Jews did not live there, though at times they numbered no more than a handful. Today, since the return of the Jewish people to its land, and particularly since Jerusalem's reunification after the Six Day War in 1967, the city has become a true center for Jewish institutions and organizations. Educational institutions of every sort have sprung up here, particularly institutions of Jewish and religious education. Many Jews from the Diaspora visit Jerusalem as representatives of various organizations; many spend a portion of their lives here as students. In this introductory chapter, we present a portrait of the Jerusalem of today.

A Reunion in Jerusalem

As children, Judy and Susan, two Jewish girls, lived in Johannesburg, South Africa. They studied together there in a Jewish school where they became close friends. When they reached bat mitzvah age, their parents decided to leave South Africa. Judy's family settled in Toronto, Canada, and Susan's family moved to Sydney, Australia. At first, the girls corresponded, but as time passed, they lost touch with each other.

A few years later, Judy came to Israel. It was not her first time, but this time it was not just another visit. Now she was in Israel to study for a year in Jerusalem, and her parents agreed that if she wished she could continue her studies at the Hebrew University. Judy came to Israel with a group of young people from North America. Although Judy was very happy with the program, she felt lonely, as she did not know anyone else in the group. Before the beginning of the school year, the group went on several tours. One hot day in the middle of the summer, when the group was enjoying an ice cream in the park adjacent to the old Knesset building in the center of Jerusalem, another group of English speaking young people passed. Among the young women, Judy saw one whose face looked familiar. She took a closer look: Susan! The two girls shouted and hugged in their joy and excitement at meeting each other and were delighted to discover that both had come to study at the same institution, one which takes in Jewish young people from all over the world. With no previous planning, the two friends met and renewed their friendship in Jerusalem.

Ingathering of Exiles

Look, O children, from afar
City of Zion, your people lives
If to the ends of earth we wander
Our hearts yet long for you
Before your summit we came together
Brother reaching out for brother

(Shaul Tchernichovsky)

Going Up to Jerusalem - a Memoir

Rahel Yana'it Ben Tzvi immigrated to what was then Turkish Palestine as a young pioneer in 1908. She became one of the leading activists in the Zionist movement and the Haganah (the pre-state, Jewish defense organization) and married Yitzhak Ben Tzvi, later elected second president of Israel. In her memoirs, she describes her first trip to Jerusalem a short while after arriving in the country:

Light-drenched memories of my first days in Jerusalem fill my heart. I board the train to Jerusalem, and from the first moment, I am enveloped in an indescribable feeling of exaltation. In the same train car with me sits an Orthodox Jew from Jerusalem in his traditional dress, and next to him an Arab, resplendent in black with a red tarbush on his head, his entire bearing proclaiming his importance. . . .

Suddenly a Jew sitting behind me addresses me: "Why are you so happy?" he asks, "The Effendi asks why you are so happy."

He explains the reason for my happiness to the Effendi, that I am going up to Jerusalem, and everyone knows that a Jew's heart is happy when he goes up to Jerusalem.

(Rahel Yana'it Ben Tzvi, Anu Olim)

The train to Jerusalem

1000

1996

*"We must make
Jerusalem the center of the
entire Jewish people. . . .
Jerusalem has always been and must remain the
heart of the Jewish people."*

David Ben Gurion

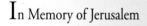

A square cubit of a Jerusalem house, left unpainted in memory of the destruction of the Temple

מקדש אור חמדתי זכור זכרתיהו

ועל ראש שמחתי
בין עיני שמתיהו

ומכתלי ביתי
נכר כי שחרתיהו

In Memory of Jerusalem

From the time the Jews went into exile, they developed various ways of remembering Jerusalem. In the Shulhan Arukh, the standard code of Jewish law, we find:

From the time the Temple was destroyed, the Sages legislated that we never erect a building decorated with pictures but rather finish all buildings with simple plaster and paint and leave a square cubit opposite the entrance unpainted (in memory of the destruction of the Temple).

When a man marries a woman, he takes a bit of ash and smears it on his forehead. . ., and in some communities he breaks a glass under the bridal canopy. . . .

All these measures are taken to remember Jerusalem, as is written, "If I forget thee, O Jerusalem, may my right hand forget its cunning" (Psalms 137:5). . . .

(Shulhan Arukh, Orah Hayyim 560:1-2)

"Every Jew carries his own Jerusalem within his heart."

(Levi Eshkol)

-1000

0

View from a Sidewalk Cafe in the Heart of Jerusalem

You can learn much about Jerusalem from a visit to her sites and institutions, her archaeological monuments and museums. But you can learn every bit as much about the city - and with a lot less effort - just by stopping for coffee and cake in one of the many sidewalk cafes on Ben Yehuda Street.

Ben Yehudah Street runs right through the center of downtown Jerusalem. A few years ago it was closed to traffic and repaved in stone. In English, Ben Yehuda Street is now called the Downtown Mall. In Hebrew, they call it the Midrahov.

We sat there recently, my wife and I, and watched the crowds of people passing by without break: native Jerusalemites and their guests, Jews and non-Jews, the average and the curious - you find all of them on the Midrahov. Here is a group of black-skinned men and women: tourists from some African nation? From the United States? Or perhaps new immigrants from Ethiopia? While we try to discover the answer, two Hasidim pass by in their long black robes. They pass quickly looking neither right nor left, immersed in their own world. Opposite us stands an older man, singing and accompanying himself on the violin.

Next to him is a hand-written sign, "This is my work." He is a new immigrant, who, failing to find employment in his field, decided to support himself by playing music here on the Midrahov. Since he's been doing it for several years now, he seems to be making a living. Now a group of people has collected around him, all of them wearing identical shirts bearing some message. My wife strains to read: "Jewish Volunteers from Canada." Two policewomen join the circle. Next to them passes an Arab and with him two women decked out from head to toe in black garments and white head coverings. Two nuns approach, they, too, are completely covered in black but with large crosses dangling from their necks. Behind them stands a family with children

Views of the Jerusalem Midrahov

Jerusalem - Focus of Negotiations for Peace

of different ages, hungrily eyeing the pizza and falafel stands. A noisy group of high school girls crowds into a jewelry store. They pay no attention to the strange skinny man in rumpled clothing who passes by, carrying a sign on which are written the words, "THE TORAH SAYS: JERUSALEM BELONGS TO THE JEWISH PEOPLE ONLY."

On the Midrahov you can hear all languages and taste cuisine of every origin. On the Midrahov, you can meet anyone, even someone from Afula or Brazil. From the sidewalk cafes, you can see and feel the Jerusalem of three religions, the international Jerusalem, and more than anything else, Jewish Jerusalem in all its variety.

Today, as so many times in the past, Jerusalem is at the center of a great controversy. Since the signing of the Declaration of Principles on 12 September 1993 ("the Oslo agreement"), Jerusalem finds herself the focus of discussion between Israel and the Palestinians concerning the permanent settlement between the two peoples.

Israel sees the united Jerusalem as the eternal capital of the Jewish people and is not prepared to see the city divided again. The Palestinians, on the other hand, view the eastern portion of Jerusalem as the capital of the Palestinian state they wish to establish.

Is Jerusalem destined to become a symbol of peace between Jews and Arabs or remain a bone of bitter contention?

The Midrahov

-1000

0

There Is No Place Like Jerusalem

There is no place like Jerusalem
City of seers and God;
One are you, Jerusalem
Heart of the holy land.

There is no place like Jerusalem
Glory of many peoples
One are you, Jerusalem
Our soul goes out to you.

There is no place like Jerusalem
City holy to all
One are you, Jerusalem
Ours for ever more.

(Avraham Broides)

The Jerusalem Shuttle

Joseph Pinto owns a travel agency in a large city in South America. His city is the home of a small, but enthusiastic, Jewish community. In spite of its small Jewish population, there is plenty of activity, and at the center of it all you'll find Joseph Pinto and his wife Alice. We bumped into Joseph on the Midrahov in Jerusalem. "Nu, Joseph, in Jerusalem again?"

"Yes, recently, it seems that all I do is travel back and forth. They ought to make me an honorary board member of the airline. Three months ago, I was here for a conference of heads of Latin American Jewish communities. A month and a half ago, there was a conference to encourage Jewish tourism. In another two months, the Jewish Agency will be holding a discussion on the problems of educating Jewish youth."

"And now?"

"This time I'm accompanying my wife. She's president of the Hadassah chapter in our city, and she has an important international conference here."

"Where are you staying?"

"Well, you know, we don't stay in hotels anymore. I got sick of being in a different place every time I came. My son got married and made aliyah; he's living in Jerusalem. I'm here almost as much as I'm at home. So we bought a little apartment, where we stay every time we come now. Believe me, it's not often empty!"

1000

1996

Jerusalem the Crowded

Those who live in Jerusalem, and even those who are only visiting, often encounter all sorts of events connected to the city's being the capital of Israel. A wide variety of governmental and Jewish programs are conducted in Jerusalem. On the one hand, all this activity makes the city an interesting place to be. On the other hand, it can be quite a nuisance. Whoever planned the city center a hundred or so years ago - and it appears that no one planned it! - certainly did not consider that the city might need a boulevard for parades, as in ancient Babylon and in modern-day Paris. Narrow, twisting Jaffa Road, Jerusalem's Main Street, is far from being suited to the throngs of marchers that frequent it, particularly during the holidays, but on regular week days as well. Who comes to march in Jerusalem? Athletic organizations, youth movements, army units, friends of Israel from foreign countries, demonstrators for and against the government, etc., etc., etc. The list of who doesn't come would probably be shorter. When there's no parade, there must certainly be some president, king, or prime minister coming to visit - another reason for Jerusalem's finest to dutifully close all the main arteries. And when Jaffa Road is closed, all Jerusalem is paralyzed. Cars stop moving and the city turns into a giant traffic jam. The poor policemen have to work for hours after to get the city unsnarled. May God have mercy on anyone with the bad luck of having to get to work or get home when the President of Upper Volta comes to visit or when the Mothers Against Artificial Food Coloring have their demonstration. If you're lucky, you won't be stuck more than two or three hours.

Dancers parade through the center of Jerusalem

At the entrance to Jerusalem, you can always find signs welcoming various Jewish and non-Jewish organizations holding their conventions here:

Jerusalem welcomes WIZO women, Jerusalem welcomes Hapo'el, Jerusalem welcomes B'nei Akiva, The Zionist Congress, The World Conference Of Rabbis, The World Union Of Jewish Students, etc., etc., etc.

I've always wondered whether the municipal government has a storeroom somewhere, where they keep all these signs, or maybe, the city has a whole mini-staff of busy workers who do nothing but paint them.

12

A Torah Center in Modern Times

Prayer notes in the Western Wall

Years ago, when a difficult problem of Jewish law arose in one of the Jewish communities of the Diaspora, the local rabbi would describe the problem in a letter, and when a group of merchants would leave for a city with an important yeshiva, the rabbi would send his query and wait for a response from the yeshiva's scholars. Sometimes, he might wait a full year for an answer until the merchants returned.

Today, the international center of Torah scholarship is Jerusalem with her many yeshivot and religious institutions. When a rabbi somewhere in South America or the Far East has a problem, he mails his letter by fax. Today, you can even fax a note to be inserted in the Western Wall. Those ancient stones which have seen so much are witness in our time to the wonders of modern technology.

Torah study at Yeshivat Har Etzion

1996

1000

Events in the Life of Jerusalem

The Israeli Supreme Court

Anyone who explores Jerusalem will be surrounded by structures and ruins that testify to the city's rich history: days of glory and ruin, periods when Jerusalem served as the center of a Jewish kingdom, and periods when hardly any Jews lived here. Alongside the Knesset and the Israel Museum, the new neighborhoods that surround the city - all modern structures of our own period - you can find synagogues built hundreds of years ago; churches of every Christian denomination and numerous mosques; monuments commemorating battles and losses from the time of Israel's War of Independence and the Six Day War; and foundations of buildings and streets from Roman times. Jerusalem also contains mysterious tombs of people from biblical times - Absalom son of David and the prophetess Hulda - as well as tombs of important people from every generation, including renowned sages from the furthest reaches of the Diaspora - from Italy, Eastern Europe, Morocco, and Yemen. Important figures from recent generations, such as Eliezer Ben Yehudah and Theodore Herzl, are also buried here. The names of Jerusalem's streets tell the history of the Jewish people in all periods and places, from the prophet Isaiah and the medieval Bible commentator Nahmanides to the murdered Herzl Baazov, a Zionist leader from the Soviet Republic of Georgia.

Meeting place for Jews the world over; object of Jewish longing throughout the generations; cosmopolitan tourist attraction and center of three religions; host to conventions, congresses, parades, and demonstrations; busy, overcrowded capital of a modern nation-state; center of Jewish piety and scholarship; and burial ground for the central figures of Jewish history - Jerusalem is greater than the sum of its parts.

We hope that this booklet will spark your interest in visiting Jerusalem and getting to know the eternal capital of the Jewish people on intimate terms.

Views of old and new Jerusalem

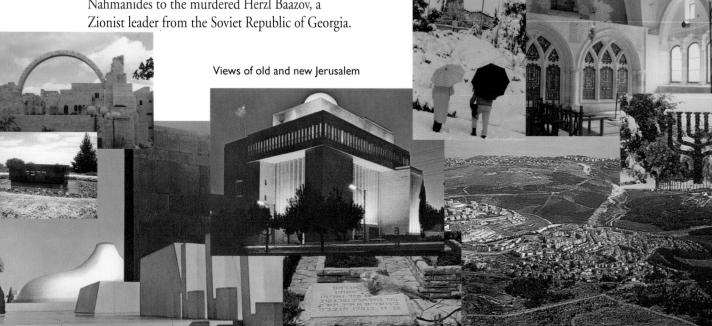

DAVID MAKES JERUSALEM
THE CAPITAL OF ISRAEL

David Conquers Jerusalem

"Nevertheless, David took the stronghold of Zion the City of David. . . And David dwelt in the stronghold" (II Samuel 5:7, 9).

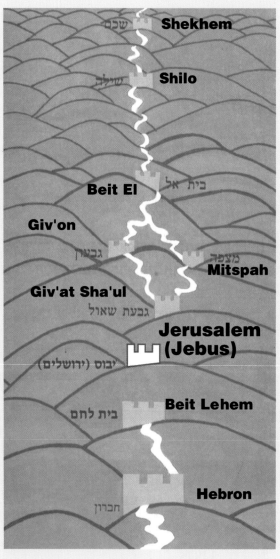

The strategic position of Jerusalem in King David's time

David's reign began in Hebron, which served as his capital for seven years. Later, he decided that the city best suited to be the center of his kingdom was Jerusalem. David chose Jerusalem for two reasons. First, the Children of Israel held the entire central mountain range; only Jerusalem, city of the Jebusites, remained in the hands of a foreign people. Jerusalem thus divided the tribes of Israel in the North from the tribes of Judea in the South. Second, Hebron belonged to David's own tribe, the tribe of Judah. David needed a capital not identified with one tribe or another. Jerusalem, then, had two advantages, her central location and her neutrality in not belonging to any particular tribe.

-1004

0

Jerusalem was well fortified, her walls impenetrable. Her Jebusite inhabitants mocked David's forces. "Even the blind and the crippled could repulse you," they shouted down from Jerusalem's forbidding walls. David answered with a solemn promise that the first to breach the wall would become a leader of the Israeli nation.

Jebusite Jerusalem as David saw it (Reconstruction)

Legend tells that Joab son of Tzeruyah, commander of David's army cut a young pine tree, bent it backwards, and catapulted himself into the city. The courageous fighter's sudden appearance inside the walls created such confusion that David and his men were able to scale the walls and follow. And that is how Jerusalem fell.
(II Samuel 5:6; I Chronicles 11:6; Midrash Tehilim 18:24)

Jerusalem was conquered and became the capital of Israel in the year 1,004 B.C.E., some 3,000 years ago.

17

1000   2000

David Purchases the Temple Mount and Jerusalem

After conquering Jerusalem, David did not destroy the city or raise his hand against her Jebusite inhabitants. Nor did he wish to acquire Jerusalem for the Jewish people only by virtue of conquest. David therefore decided to purchase the city for its full price and grant every Jew a share. Each tribe contributed fifty shekels, and David matched their contributions with his own.

The Midrash tells: "And afterward, he purchased the city from the Jebusites for the Jewish people as an everlasting possession with an irrevocable deed." (Pirkei deRabbi Eliezer 36).

Nor was David satisfied to take the Temple Mount by military conquest. He purchased the Temple Mount from its owner, Aravnah the Jebusite. The Bible tells that when David decided to purchase land for the Temple, Aravnah wished to give him the land as a gift, but David would not agree: "No, I will buy it from you" (II Samuel 24:24). And so it was. Thus David followed in the footsteps of Abraham our father, who paid full price for the burial cave of Makhpelah.

Abraham and Isaac by Rembrandt (1606-1669)

H ow did David know where the Temple would be built?

The Midrash tells that David was pained at not knowing which site was suitable for the Temple and that God sent the prophet Gad to show him. It was a venerable site, made holy by the ancients. According to Tradition, the same site was used for sacrifice by Adam and by Noah when he left the ark, and it was the site where Abraham bound his beloved Isaac to the sacrificial altar. Again, according to Tradition, David himself surveyed the Temple Mount, calculating the exact site of the Holy of Holies and the altar.
(Pesikta Rabbati 43)

David Makes Jerusalem His Capital

After conquering Jerusalem, David made her the capital city of Israel. In Jerusalem, he established the institutions of his rule. Jerusalem became the seat of the army high command and of the royal officials responsible for the economy, taxes, government functions, and the royal court. David himself was the supreme judge, hearing cases brought by the people. David had the Holy Ark brought to Jerusalem from Kiryat Ya'arim, thus transforming the city into a spiritual center as well.

It was also his intention to build the Temple to reinforce Jerusalem's role as the center of the Jewish people and the land of Israel, but he did not receive God's permission. David was denied this privilege because of his military activities; it would not have been fitting for a man of war to build the Temple, cornerstone of peace in this world. David himself tells of his disappointment:

1000

2000

"But the word of the Lord came to me, saying: You have shed blood abundantly, and made great wars; you shall not build a house unto My name. . . Behold, a son shall be born to you, who shall be a man of peace. . . He shall build a house for My name. . ."
(I Chronicles 22:8-10).

Prevented from building the Temple himself, David, nevertheless, prepared the raw materials, and according to Tradition, dug the foundations.

King David the Psalmist, Rothschild Miscellany, Northern Italy 1450-1470

Legend tells of David's days and nights. A harp hung above David's bed. When the north wind blew, its strings would vibrate and play a melody, awakening the composer. At dawn, the leaders of the Children of Israel, the commanders of his army, and the high royal officials would come to him. These would counsel with David and seek his decisions on affairs of the realm: economic and military matters, religion, law. During the day, David attended to the needs of people and the state. His nights were dedicated to praise and supplication.
II Samuel 7; 8:16-18; I Chronicles 22-28; Babylonian Talmud, Berakhot 3b

-1004

0

David's Emblem: The Man and the City

In his youth, David had been a shepherd. Later he achieved greatness and was anointed king of Israel. Among his greatest deeds were conquering Jerusalem and transforming her into the everlasting capital of Israel.

The Midrash tells that, as is the custom of kings, David selected an emblem to be imprinted on coins, buildings, and official documents. The emblem he chose testifies both to David's humility and his recognition of Jerusalem's significance for all generations. On one side of his emblem appeared a shepherd's staff and satchel, reminder of David's early days as a shepherd; on the other side a tower, symbol of Jerusalem which David captured and fortified.
(Midrash Rabbah, Bereshit 39, 16)

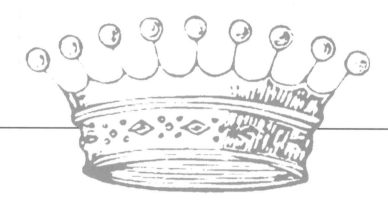

A folk story passed down by the Jews of Iraq tells of a country with a unique procedure for choosing its monarch. It seems that when the king died, in the capital city they would release a bird known as the Bird of Happiness. The person on whom the Bird of Happiness perched would be appointed king.

Once it happened that the bird perched on the head of a slave, whose work it was to play a drum and dance at weddings while wearing a hat of feathers. The slave was taken to the palace, dressed in royal robes, and a crown was placed upon his head. From that day forth, he reigned as king.

The new king requested of his servants to erect a small hut right outside his opulent palace. In the hut, he kept his drum and his hat of feathers, and on the wall, he hung a large mirror. From time to time, the king would go to the hut, put on his hat, take up his drum, play it and dance.

His ministers wondered what their king did inside the hut. When they followed him and discovered his odd behavior, the ministers told the king that it was unseemly for a king to behave so, even if none of his subjects saw him. But the king replied:
"When I see myself in the mirror, I remember that I was a slave, and thus I remind myself that I am no better than other men. This is how I protect myself from pride."

(Dov Noy, Folktales of Israel)

David's emblem reflects a similar idea.

-1004

0

The Eternal Bond Between David and Jerusalem

King David's tomb on Mount Zion

David died in Jerusalem, but no one knows where he was buried. According to a popular tradition, his tomb is on Mount Zion. The people never resigned themselves to David's death but linked him, rather, in various ways to the future Redemption: According to popular belief, the future Messiah will be a scion of the house of David. In our prayers, we mention David and pray for renewal of his kingdom: "Return in mercy to thy city Jerusalem. . . Rebuild it soon, in our days. . ., and speedily establish in it the throne of David. . . ." (the Amidah prayer). According to the Midrash, David prayed that his psalms would always be recited by the Jewish people. David asked, "Master of the Universe, may I merit that my psalms be forever recited in houses of study and prayer."

(Jerusalem Talmud, Shekalim 2:7; Midrash Tehilim 30:3)

Many of David's psalms sing of Jerusalem and the Temple:

I rejoiced when they said to me, "Let us go to the house of the Lord." Now we stand within your gates, O Jerusalem - Jerusalem that is built to be a city where people come together in unity, to which the tribes resort, the tribes of the Lord, to give thanks to the Lord himself, the bounden duty of Israel. For in her are set the thrones of justice, the thrones of the house of David. Pray for the peace of Jerusalem: "May those who love you prosper; peace be within your ramparts and prosperity in your palaces." For the sake of these my brothers and my friends, I will say, "Peace be within you." For the sake of the house of the Lord our God, I will pray for your good.
(Psalms 122)

23

1000

2000

The Name Jerusalem

Yisrael Najara, a Hebrew poet who lived in the land of Israel towards the end of the sixteenth century, writes in one of his poems:

Bring me to the city of Zion
And redeem her from siege
Let my leader reign in my city
Let the son of Jesse reign

Let him return to his former glory
As in ancient days long past
Let him restore the Levite to his rightful place
And the Kohen to his service

(R. Yisrael Najara, excerpts from Zemirot Yisrael)

City of David

By the light of day it is but a village
Enveloped in the odor of smoke
And ordure.
Ah, but at night. When its lights come to life
With a young girl's laugh
I am born anew at her feet,
And like my father's father's
Young father
At midnight
I hear it playing
David's harp.

(Zerubavel Gilead)

From the time the Jebusite city was conquered by David, it has been known in Jewish sources by the name Jerusalem. So it is known to Christians as well. The source of the Hebrew name, Yerushalayim, is not altogether clear. Historians suggest that the city's original name was Shalem, and that Shalem was the name of a person or some ancient god. Another theory holds the name Yerushalayim to be derived from the word for peace, shalom. To the root name, shalem or shalom the Sumerian word uru, city, may have been added, making the name City of Shalem or City of Shalom.

The Sages of the Talmud offer another explanation: Abraham called the site Yireh (or Jireh in English; Genesis 22:14), which means "God will see and protect the city." Shem, son of Noah, called the same site Shalem (or Salem in English), which means whole, complete, or perfect. From these two names, our Sages tell us, the name Yerushalayim - Jerusalem - was formed.
(Midrash Rabbah, Bereshit 56:16)

Another explanation is that the name Yerushalayim is derived from the words yerushah le'olam, an eternal possession. According to this view, the name Yerushalayim implies that Jerusalem will belong to the Jewish people forever.

SOLOMON STRENGTHENS JERUSALEM AS A POLITICAL AND RELIGIOUS CENTER

SOLOMON STRENGTHENS JERUSALEM AS A POLITICAL AND RELIGIOUS CENTER

Solomon Consolidates His Kingdom

And Solomon was king over all Israel.
And Solomon ruled over all the kingdoms from the
[Euphrates] River to the land of the Philistines, and to
the border of Egypt; they brought presents and served
Solomon all the days of his life. And Solomon sent to
Hiram, saying, "Behold, I intend to build a house for
the name of the Lord, my God."
(I Kings 4:1, 5:1, 5:16, 5:19).

Jerusalem in the days of Solomon
.... Wall of the present-day Old City

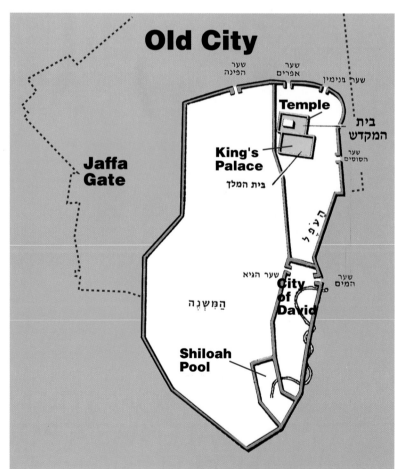

-960

0

SOLOMON STRENGTHENS JERUSALEM AS A POLITICAL AND RELIGIOUS CENTER

Solomon reigned in the land of Israel from about 970 B.C.E. From his father, King David, he inherited a large kingdom located at the intersection of important trade routes connecting the Arabian Peninsula, Egypt, and Syria. During Solomon's reign, the country was at peace: "And Judah and Israel dwelt safely, every man under his vine and under his fig tree, from Dan to Beersheba, all the days of Solomon" (I Kings 5:5). Solomon created an administrative structure for the country, dividing it into regions, appointing governors, and levying taxes. He established relations with neighboring rulers - particularly with Hiram, King of Tyre - and developed commerce. Great wealth flowed into the country. Solomon's income from taxes and trade supported an extensive program of construction throughout the land. Great fortified storage cities were built at Hatzor, Megiddo and Gezer, to protect the country against invaders.

Solomon invested considerable effort and tremendous financial resources in the capital city of Jerusalem. He built numerous buildings, city walls, and a beautiful imperial palace, using the best grades of stone and cedars imported from Lebanon. In its central hall stood a throne of ivory. While the palace served as the center of Solomon's regime, his crowning achievement was the Temple.

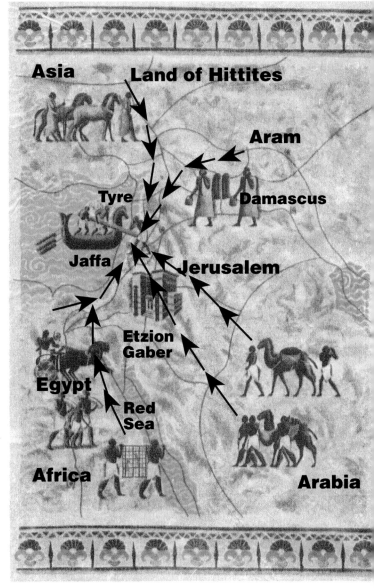

Trade routes in King Solomon's time

Building the Temple

The First Temple (artist's conception)

The Temple was an extraordinarily beautiful structure fashioned from the most expensive materials - gold and brass, precious stones, cedar wood; the work was carried out by skilled craftsmen. The completed edifice made so strong an impression on whomsoever saw it that fabulous legends grew up around its construction.

One legend has it that the enormous stones from which the walls were constructed rose by themselves to the required height and arranged themselves in rows.

The Bible tells that the Temple's windows were both "transparent and opaque" (I Kings 6:4), an apparent contradiction. The Rabbis resolve this contradiction by explaining that the windows were designed in an unusual fashion. Usually, windows are broad on the outside and narrow on the inside so that sufficient light can penetrate. In the Temple, however, the windows were narrow on the outside and broad on the inside, to symbolize that light went forth from the Temple to illuminate the entire world.

To preserve the Temple's sanctity, measures were taken to prevent birds from sitting on its roof and dirtying it. On the Temple roof was a net with four hundred tiny golden bells attached. When a bird would try to perch there, the bells would ring and scare it away.
(Pesikta Rabbati 6; Tanhuma Beha'alotkha 2; Ze'ev Vilnay, Agaddot Eretz Yisrael)

Ivory Pomegranate - First Temple remnant, Israel Museum

-960

0

The Temple in Jerusalem - Symbol of Peace

Priests offering incense on the altar (artist's conception)

David was not permitted to build the Temple, for he was a man of war who had shed much blood. God told David that his son would build the Temple, ". . . for his name shall be Solomon, and I will give peace and quietness to Israel in his days" (I Chronicles 22:9). We find the idea of peace in many other sources concerning Jerusalem.

Concerning the Temple, we read, ". . . and there was neither hammer nor axe nor any tool of iron heard in the house while it was in building" (I Kings 6:7). A similar verse is found in the Torah in connection with the altar built on Mount Eval: "And there you shall build an altar to the Lord your God, an altar of stones; you shall lift no iron tool upon them" (Deuteronomy 27:5). Why was it forbidden to use · · iron in the construction of the altar and the Temple?

The Sages of the Mishnah answer: "Iron was created to shorten man's life, and the altar was created to lengthen it. It would be improper to use that which shortens life upon that which lengthens life." This refers to the use of iron in the manufacture of swords, arrows, and spears - the instruments of war. According to our Sages, by the prohibition against using iron in construction, the Temple and the altar transmit the message of peace.

This same idea is found in the Midrash: "Thus all the work that King Solomon wrought in the house of the Lord was complete" (I Kings 7:51). The Midrash explains that not only was the work complete but all the workers were complete as well. During the construction of the Temple, not one worker died or even took sick. The structure that symbolized peace and completeness could not be the cause of death or even illness of those who toiled in its construction.

According to the Sages, even the name Jerusalem (Yerushalayim) implies peace. The name Jerusalem is a compromise between two different names given by two different persons. Abraham called the mountain where he bound Isaac for sacrifice Yireh (or Jireh in English; Genesis 22:14). Shem, son of Noah, called the same location

Shalem (or Salem in English). God said, "If I choose one name over the other, one of these righteous men will be insulted." So he joined the two together to form the name Yerushalayim - in English, Jerusalem.
(Mishnah Middot 3:4; Pesikta Rabbati 6; Midrash Rabbah Bereshit 56:16)

How Solomon Acquired the *Shamir* to Build the Temple

The Bible tells that ". . . there was neither hammer nor axe nor any tool of iron heard in the house while it was in building" (I Kings 6:7). If so, how was it possible to quarry and dress the Temple's stones? To this question as well, legend provides an answer.

Before Solomon began building the Temple, he asked the Sages how he could accomplish his task without the use of iron. They replied: "There is a tiny creature known as the shamir, and when it is placed on stone, the stone splits."

Solomon asked, "where can I find this creature?" "The shamir was given to the hoopoe bird," they replied, "and the hoopoe bird lives at the top of a mountain that is extremely difficult to scale."

Solomon chose several of his bravest soldiers and Benayahu ben Yehoyada, supreme commander of his army, to lead them. He sent them to find the hoopoe bird and to retrieve the shamir. Solomon's men walked for many days, through deserts and over mountains, until they came to the hoopoe's nest. When they arrived, the hoopoe was not there; only her young were in the nest. They took a plate of glass, covered the nest, and hid close by.

When the hoopoe arrived with seeds for her chicks, she saw that they were covered by glass. The hoopoe pecked at the glass and so did the chicks. But the glass held, separating the mother from her hungry brood. The hoopoe flew away and returned with the shamir in her beak. She placed the shamir on the glass, and the glass immediately split in half. Suddenly, Benayahu shouted in a loud voice. The hoopoe took fright and flew away, and Benayahu jumped out and grabbed the shamir. Benayahu and his men returned to Jerusalem and brought the shamir to Solomon.

Thus, when the Temple's builders needed to split a rock, they would draw a line on it in ink and place the shamir on the line; the rock would split along the marking.

(M. Y. Ben Gurion, miMekor Yisrael; Talmud Bavli, Sotah 48b)

-960

0

Solomon Makes Jerusalem a Spiritual Center

When the Temple was completed, Solomon assembled the leaders of the people and the priests, and dedicated the Temple (around 960 B.C.E.) in an impressive ceremony. He transferred the Holy Ark from where it had been kept during David's reign to its permanent place in the Temple. In a long address to the people and in a prayer to God, Solomon dedicated the structure to holy service. He called upon the people to turn to the Temple in all times of trouble, such as drought, plague, and war, and he prayed to God asking that He save His people in times of distress. At the end of the ceremony, which included the offering of numerous sacrifices, the king blessed the people, and everyone returned home "joyful and glad of heart" (I Kings 8:66).

Celebrating the Dedication of the Temple

Many generations passed, and the Temple's position as sole center of the Jewish people's worship became firmly entrenched. During this time, the prophets fought against idol worship and other cultic centers which had sprung up around the country. Solomon's initiative in building the Temple did not immediately succeed in destroying all vestiges of idol worship. However, construction of the Temple and the concentration of holy service in it did lay the foundation for Jerusalem to become the holy city of the Jewish people for all generations.

The Temple that Solomon built stood for nearly four hundred years, until it was destroyed by the Babylonians in 586 B.C.E.

Why the Temple Was Built on a Mountain Overlooking Jerusalem

It is a tradition known to all, that the place where David and Solomon built the altar, on the site of Aravnah's threshing floor, is the same place where Abraham built an altar to bind Isaac for sacrifice, the place where Noah built an altar when he came out of the ark, the place where Cain and Abel brought their offerings to God, and where Adam sacrificed after his creation. And Adam was created from the earth of that very spot.
(R. Moshe ben Maimon, Mishneh Torah, Hilkhot Beit haBehirah 2:2)

Threshing the grain harvest in the Judean Hills

Legend offers a different explanation:
Once there were two brothers - one single, the
other married with children - whose father had
bequeathed them a house and wheat fields. The
two brothers worked their fields together, and
after the harvest, they divided their grain equally.
The night after the harvest, the unmarried
brother could not sleep. He thought: "I am
single, and it is not fair that I receive the same
portion as my brother who must support a wife
and children." What did he do? He got out of bed
and went to the field, where he took several of his
sheaves and placed them with his brother's.

The married brother also had trouble sleeping
that night. He thought to himself: "My brother is
not married. He needs to find a wife and build a
home. It is not fair that I receive as much as he."
What did he do? He got out of bed and went to
the field, where he took several of his sheaves and
placed them with his brother's.

When the brothers arose in the morning, each
was surprised to discover that his portion was the
same size as when he had gone to bed the night
before. Both, therefore, repeated the same deed
the following night, and again on the third night.
On the third night they met, however, each one
carrying a sheaf he intended to move to his
brother's portion of the property.

That same night Solomon went out for a
midnight stroll. Solomon understood the language
of animals, and he heard a small bird telling her
friend of the generosity of the two brothers.
Solomon went to the field and met the two
brothers, who were embracing in brotherly love.
Upon seeing them, Solomon recited a verse from
one of his father's psalms, "Behold, how good and
pleasant it is for brothers to dwell together"
(Psalms 133:1). Solomon purchased the field
from the two brothers. There is no better place, he
thought, than this site of brotherly love, to build
the Temple.
(Folk legend as told by the Jews of Morocco;
Chaim Schwartzbaum, Shorashim veNofim)

-960

0

SOLOMON STRENGTHENS JERUSALEM AS A POLITICAL AND RELIGIOUS CENTER

Solomon's Wisdom

The members of Solomon's generation believed their king to be possessed of extraordinary wisdom: "And Solomon's wisdom was very great. . . . For he was wiser than all men. . ." (I Kings 5:10-11). The Bible tells of his ability to solve complex legal problems (such as the case of two women both of whom claimed to be the mother of the same baby; I Kings 3:16ff) and to solve the riddles presented him by the Queen of Sheba (I Kings 10:1). Two of the Wisdom Books of the Bible, Proverbs and Ecclesiastes, are attributed to Solomon, as is the Song of Songs.

Here are three sayings taken from Solomon's writings:

"Better a dry crust and harmony than a house full of feasting and strife"
(Proverbs 17:1).

"What has happened will happen again, and what has been done will be done again, and there is nothing new under the sun"
(Ecclesiastes 1:9).

". . . For love is as strong as death, jealousy - cruel as the grave"
(Song of Songs 8:6).

The Judgement of Solomon by William Dyce (1806-1864)

1000   2000

According to the Bible, Solomon's wisdom was so well known that the Queen of Sheba, Queen of a large, important kingdom located in present-day Ethiopia, journeyed to Jerusalem especially to speak with Solomon on matters of wisdom, or, as is written, "to test him with hard questions" (I Kings 10:1). According to a Yemenite midrash, some of the questions that the Queen of Sheba put to Solomon were about the Bible - the first Bible quiz in history. So, for instance, the Queen of Sheba is said to have asked Solomon where in the Bible it is told that three went into a cave and emerged as five. Solomon replied that the answer lies in the nineteenth chapter of Genesis, where it is told that Lot went into a cave with his two daughters, where each one conceived a child.

The Queen of Sheba being received by Solomon, Sir Edward Poynter (1839-1919)

 SOLOMON STRENGTHENS JERUSALEM AS A POLITICAL AND RELIGIOUS CENTER

A folk tradition tells that, in spite of his greatness and wealth, and although his reign was blessed with peace, Solomon would sometimes become depressed and sink into anxiety and worry. To overcome his moods, he had a goldsmith fashion a ring for him on which were engraved the Hebrew letters gimmel, zayin, yud, the first letters of the Hebrew words gam zeh ya'avor - this too will pass. From that time, whenever Solomon's mood darkened, he would gaze upon his ring and be encouraged.

(Folk tale of the Sephardi Jews. Matilda Koen-Sarano, Kuentos)

The Role of the Temple in the Life of the People

The Torah commands: "Three times in a year shall all your males appear before the Lord your God in the place which He shall choose: on the feast of Passover, and on the feast of Shavuot, and on the feast of Sukkot" (Deuteronomy 16:16). The three feasts mentioned here are the three pilgrimage holidays. From the time that Solomon erected the First Temple, Jerusalem became the spiritual center of the Jewish people, where the people came on the pilgrimage holidays to sacrifice and celebrate God's beneficence. For generations following Solomon, however, the people remained divided; many were those who made their pilgrimage to other holy sites. Nevertheless, construction of the Temple by Solomon laid the foundation for the role of Jerusalem and the Temple during the Second Temple period, when thousands of Jews from all over the country and from countries of the Diaspora gathered in Jerusalem throughout the year, and particularly on feasts and holidays.

Pilgrims on their way to the Temple

Jerusalem and the Temple play a central role in the consciousness of the Jewish people, and this is clearly manifest in our prayers. The liturgy contains numerous verses such as:

Bring us in joy to Zion, Your city, and to Jerusalem, Your Temple, in eternal happiness.

May it be Your will, O Lord our God. . . to return and take pity upon us and the Temple in Your great mercy, and rebuild it speedily.

(Liturgy of the High Holy Days).

These prayers played an important role in preserving the connection between the people and its land during the thousands of years of exile, and were the soil in which modern Zionism took root.

THE PEOPLE RETURN TO ZION -
JERUSALEM REBUILT

HE PEOPLE RETURN TO ZION - JERUSALEM REBUILT

Destruction of the First Temple and Babylonian Exile

The Jews were a small people in a small country surrounded by large and powerful neighbors. In the several hundred years after David and Solomon, the country was attacked many times by surrounding nations: Aram, Assyria, Egypt, Babylon. Sometimes the Jews managed to repulse the invaders, but at others, they were defeated and portions of the country conquered. The Jews' ability to resist military incursions diminished greatly after the death of Solomon, when his kingdom was divided in two: the southern kingdom of Judah, comprising the tribes of Judah and Benjamin, and the northern kingdom of Israel, comprising the other ten tribes. In addition to wars with foreign powers, the two Jewish mini-kingdoms often found themselves at war with each other. Naturally, this internal fighting further diminished their ability to withstand threats from the outside.

Jerusalem in the days of Nehemiah

━━ Wall of the present-day Old City

-516

-1000   0

Reading the book of Lamentations (Eicha) on the Ninth of Av

In the year 722 B.C.E., Israel, the northern kingdom, was conquered by the Assyrians. To prevent the residents from rebelling, the conquerors exiled many of them, dispersing them among distant countries.

Since then, many legends have grown up about distant peoples (for instance, the Pathans in Afghanistan) alleged to be descended from the Israelite tribes sent into exile.

The Babylonian Exile, wall plaque

The kingdom of Judah managed to survive for several more generations, but in 586 B.C.E. it, too, fell to Nebuchadnezzar, King of Babylon. Jerusalem and the Temple were destroyed, and many of the residents of Judah exiled. The Temple's precious vessels were plundered and taken to the royal palace in Babylon.

Jewish Life in Babylon and Longing for Zion

The exiles of the northern kingdom were scattered among various nations and, as time passed, assimilated among foreign peoples. The exiles from Judah, however, were permitted to settle together in Babylon, where they organized themselves into communities not very different from today's Jewish communities in the Diaspora. The communities had their own leadership, rabbis, synagogues, charitable and educational institutions. The Jews worked at farming and crafts, and many managed to become firmly established economically.

Mourning the destruction of Jerusalem by the rivers of Babylon, by Ephraim Lilien

The Jews exiled to Babylon did not forget the land of Israel or Jerusalem. They remembered the words of the prophet Jeremiah, who not only prophesied the destruction and exile but witnessed them with his own eyes. Speaking in God's name, Jeremiah had promised: ". . .I will gather you again from all the nations and all the places to which I have banished you, says the Lord, and bring you back to the place from which I have carried you into exile" (Jeremiah 29:14).

The Bible tells of Daniel, one of the Babylonian exiles and a scion of an important Judean family. In many ways, Daniel typified the Jews who settled in Babylon, their successful adaptation to the new environment, their longing for their lost homeland. Daniel served in the royal court of Babylon, but prayed in his home facing windows that opened towards Jerusalem (Daniel 6:11). Psalm 137 (verses 1 and 6) reveals something of the feelings of the exiles:

By the rivers of Babylon, we sat down and wept when we remembered Zion. If I forget you, O Jerusalem, let my right hand forget its cunning; let my tongue cleave to the roof of my mouth if I do not remember you, if I do not set Jerusalem above my highest joy.

-516

-1000   0

Punishment for those who Destroyed Jerusalem

The Jews of Babylon believed they were exiled from their land as a consequence of their sins but that, nevertheless, they remained God's chosen people. God, they were convinced, would have mercy upon them and return them to the land of Israel. The Babylonians, God's instrument for punishing the Jews, were themselves punished for all they had done to the land and the people. Nebuchadnezzar's son Belshazzar, last of the Babylonian monarchs, lost his kingdom as a consequence of his acts against the Jewish people and the holiness of the Temple.

One day, Belshazzar held a great celebration for a thousand of his royal officials. At that feast, the revelers praised their pagan god while drinking wine from golden vessels that Nebuchadnezzar had plundered from the Temple in Jerusalem. As they drank, a human hand appeared and wrote a message on the wall of the banquet hall in some unknown alphabet. The king was frightened and sought someone who could read the handwriting on the wall. In the end, Daniel was brought, as the message was in Aramaic, a language written in Hebrew characters and spoken by Babylon's Jews. Daniel read the message to the king:

And these are the words of the writing which was inscribed: Mene mene tekel ufarsin. Here is the interpretation: mene: God has numbered the days of your kingdom and brought it to an end; tekel: you have been weighed in the balance and found wanting; ufarsin: and your kingdom has been divided and given to the Medes and Persians.

That very night, Belshazzar was slain, and his kingdom overrun.
(Daniel, chapter 5)

The Feast of Belshazzar by Rembrandt, 1635

Cyrus's Declaration and the Jews' Return to the Land of Israel

Cyrus was the King of the conquering Persians. In order to win the loyalty of the Babylonian empire's many peoples, he proclaimed religious freedom for all. Various peoples whose temples had been damaged or destroyed by the Babylonians were permitted to reinstitute their worship. In the year 538 B.C.E., some fifty years after the destruction of the First Temple, Cyrus published a proclamation to the Jews of his kingdom:

This is the word of Cyrus of Persia: The Lord the God of Heaven has given me all the kingdoms of the earth, and he himself has charged me to build him a house at Jerusalem in Judah. To every man of his people now among you I say, God be with him, and let him go up to Jerusalem in Judah, and rebuild the house of the Lord the God of Israel, the God whose city is Jerusalem. And every remaining Jew, wherever he may be living, may claim aid from his neighbors in that place, silver and gold, goods and cattle in addition to the voluntary offerings for the house of God in Jerusalem (Ezra 1:2-4).

The Declaration of Cyrus, written on clay tablet.
539 B.C.E. (Replica)

Following Cyrus's proclamation, some fifty thousand Jewish exiles, who received considerable assistance from their fellow Jews, returned to the land of Israel. The returnees took with them Temple vessels, restored to them by Cyrus from the Babylonian royal treasury. Owing to the difficulty of crossing the desert, the returnees took an indirect route, first to the north along the River Euphrates and afterward southward via Syria. They settled in Jerusalem and its environs and began farming and simultaneously rebuilding the Temple. Additional returnees arrived later.

The first group of exiles returning to Jerusalem was headed by Zerubavel son of Shalti'el, a descendant of King David.

Exiles returning to Jerusalem, wall plaque

-516

-1000   0

One verse of the well known Hanukah song, Rock of Ages (Ma'oz Tzur), mentions Zerubavel and the return to Zion:

Soon Babylon's end drew near.
Guided by Zerubavel,
I was saved after seventy years.

The seventy years mentioned in the song are the seventy years that elapsed between destruction of the First Temple in 586 B.C.E. and completion of the Second Temple in 516 B.C.E.

Temple implements, Perpignan Bible, 1299

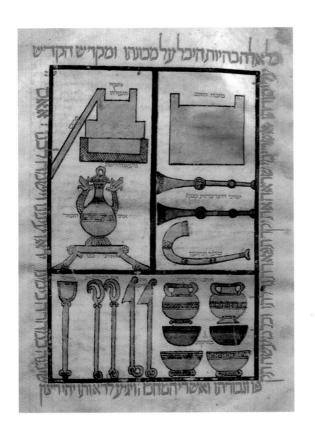

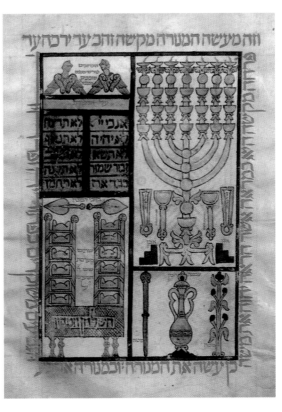

1000

2000

Building the Second Temple

With the help of money they brought from Babylon, the returning exiles constructed the Second Temple. First they built the altar; thus, shortly after their arrival, they were able to resume the offering of sacrifices. Despite a break of seventy years in the Temple service, the returnees felt the Second Temple to be the direct continuation of the First. This is clear from the legend that after the altar was constructed, a problem arose.

The Torah prohibits the use of "strange fire" for the offering of sacrifices. The first fire upon the altar came down from heaven in the days of Moses and was kept alive continuously until the First Temple was destroyed. From where would the proper fire come for the altar of the Second Temple? Among the returnees was a very old priest who in his youth had served in the First Temple and had been present on the day of the destruction. He remembered that the prophet Jeremiah had taken the fire from the altar and hidden it in a deep pit. And indeed, when they found the pit, which was covered by a great boulder, they found the eternal fire miraculously still burning after so many years, and they brought it to the Temple.

The builders continued their work, and in two years the structure was complete. Of course, it was not nearly so impressive as the First Temple. When the young people who had never seen the First Temple shouted with joy at the completion of the Second, the old people who remembered the First Temple in all its glory could only weep.
(M. Ben Gurion, miMekor Yisrael; Ezra 3:12-13)

-516
-1000   0

Ezra and His Activity in Jerusalem

The early waves of return to the land of Israel were not an adequate foundation for a viable community. The little community numbered no more than several tens of thousands and did not give rise to capable leaders. People only looked out for themselves. There was no one who could guide the people in the religious or social spheres. Great gaps developed between the wealthy and the poor.

Ezra the Scribe, from the Codex Amiatinus, 8th Century

The kings of Persia demanded that taxes be payed, and for farmers with small plots of land, it was difficult to pay the amounts levied. In order to meet their debts, the small farmers borrowed money from the wealthy, and at first gave their fields and vineyards as security. Later, to avoid foreclosure when they couldn't repay their loans, farmers gave their sons and daughters as security, and these became slaves, to all intents and purposes, to members of the local aristocracy. No one thought any more about continuing the construction and development of Jerusalem and the Temple. In the meantime, other peoples who lived in Judea and the surrounding area harrassed the weak little community which was torn internally into social classes.

The first person to leave for the land of Israel in a desire to remedy the situation was Ezra, known as Ezra the Scribe. The title, scribe, refers to one who is knowledgeable in Torah rather than to one who copies Torah scrolls. Ezra came to Jerusalem at the head of a large group of new returnees from Babylon.

Table showing the development of the alphabet

Once in the land, Ezra enacted important regulations, primarily of a religious nature. One of his innovations was replacing the ancient Hebrew script with the Hebrew characters we know today. Ezra devoted a great deal of time to teaching Torah to the people. In particular, Ezra dealt with the problem of mixed marriages: many of the Jews had taken non-Jewish wives, beginning a process of assimilation which threatened the small community. Ezra brought this to an end.

Ezra died in the Diaspora on one of his journeys to the King of Persia. His tomb still exists near Basra on the Tigris River in southern Iraq.

The social and security problems remained to trouble the community: these problems were dealt with by Nehemiah.
(The Book of Ezra; Avraham Ben Ya'akov, Kevarim Kedoshim beBavel; Sanhedrin 21b)

-516

-1000   0

Nehemiah Builds the Walls of Jerusalem

Nehemiah was an important official in the court of King Artaxerxes of Persia. When he learned of the situation in the Holy Land, he requested that the King appoint him Governor of Judea.

Nehemiah's first act was to complete the construction of Jerusalem's walls. When he arrived, he called upon the people: "Come let us rebuild the wall of Jerusalem and be rid of the reproach" (Nehemiah 2:17), for it is a disgrace that the capital of Judea be open like a small village.

Nehemiah mobilized the whole people. Each family took upon itself to build a section of the wall. Enemies tried to disrupt the work, and the defenders were compelled to repulse them by force of arms. Part of the people stood guard while the other part worked at construction. The builders also carried weapons, in case of attack:

Nehemiah before the walls of Jerusalem by Doré

"...*With one hand they worked, and with the other they held their weapons*" (Nehemiah 4:11).

Shallum, Son of Halohesh, and his Daughters

In his description of the work on the walls of Jerusalem, Nehemiah includes a list of those who participated, for example: "The Fish Gate was built by the sons of Hassenaah. . . . Next to them, the men of Tekoa did repairs. . . . Next to them, Melatiah the Gibeonite. . . . And next Hananiah a perfumer. . . "
(Nehemiah, chapter 3).

With but one exception, the list contains the names of males only, and this is quite natural given that the work included both construction and defense. In the middle of the list, though, we find, "Next to them Shallum, son of halohesh, ruler of half the district of Jerusalem, did the repairs with the help of his daughters" (Nehemiah 3:12). Neither legend nor the biblical commentators explain why only here do we find a man working with his daughters.

It is possible, however, to speculate about this case, on the basis of the verse and what we know of attitudes current at the time. Nehemiah tells us that Shallum's father was a lohesh, a doctor - not just any doctor but the kind who cures snake bite with spells and exorcises demons. Such a doctor also healed barren women by means of incantations and amulets. But in this case, the famous lohesh of Jerusalem could not heal his own daughter-in-law, who bore his son only daughters!

This must certainly have been a source of embarassment to him and distress to his son, Shallum. But Shallum decided that he would pay no attention to the mocking. He would show everyone who he and his daughters were. On the day Nehemiah called upon the people to rebuild the walls of Jerusalem and defend the city, everyone came with their sons, and Shallum brought his daughters. Everyone saw what women of valor Shallum's daughters were - that they were every bit as capable as the men. For this reason, they were mentioned in the list of builders that Nehemiah left for all generations.

The Daughters of Shallum, Son of haLohesh

The grinding of millstones by candlelight
Who is this awake in the middle of the night?
The daughters of Shallum gone out to draw
Water from the courtyard well.

The daughters of Shallum so fair
Risen early the dough to knead
Draw water, set pot aboil,
Bring the animals their feed.

The noise of millstones grinding,
As the day of days is dawning:
For with their father on this morning
To build the city's wall they go.

Only yesterday they begged him,
"The time has come to redeem by toil.
If the Lord gave you no son,
Then let the work by us be done."

"Do not fear that people will mock,
Let us not stand by and wait,
And in the future elders will relate:
Shallum's daughters were of builder stock.

As the moon sinks ever low
And beads of dew now bathe the street,
In their eyes there is a glow
Israel shall this challenge meet!

A chance like this will not return
No enemy will dare to scoff,
For they are ready for battle's burn
The daughters of Shallum, son of the lohesh.

(M. Z. Walfovski)

Nehemiah Improves the Social Situation

Chiefs, Levites and Priests signing a Covenant

With the walls built, Nehemiah was able to direct his attention to the difficult social problems. The cooperative project of building the walls lasted for nearly two months, two months during which the wealthy worked shoulder to shoulder with the poor, creating a feeling of common destiny. Nehemiah, in the wake of his success in building the walls of Jerusalem and by virtue of his office as local Governor appointed by the King of Persia, gathered the people together and demanded that the wealthy liberate the sons and daughters of the poor, restore the land to the farmers, and cancel their debts. Here is an excerpt of the words, recorded in his memoirs, that Nehemiah addressed to the wealthy leaders of the people:

What you are doing is wrong. . . . Give back today to your debtors their fields and vineyards, their olive groves and houses as well as the income in money and in corn, new wine, and oil. "We will give them back," they promised, "and exact nothing more. We will do what you say." So, summoning the priests, I put the offenders on oath to do as they had promised. (Nehemiah 5:9-12).

In this way, by gentle persuasion - without using the authority at his disposal, but rather by appealing to the consciences of the rich - Nehemiah succeeded in bringing the members of the different classes together and uniting the people.

The activities of Zerubavel, first leader of those who returned to Jerusalem; of Ezra the Scribe, who devoted himself to the improvement of religious life; and Nehemiah, who rebuilt the walls of Jerusalem and averted exploitation of the poor, ensured the position of Jerusalem as a national-spiritual center of the Jewish people for all the generations.

JERUSALEM - CAPITAL OF
THE HASMONEAN STATE

Judea As a Vassal State with Internal Autonomy

From the return of the Babylonian exiles, towards the end of the sixth century B.C.E., and for hundreds of years after, Jerusalem was subject to the rule of foreign peoples. At first, of course, the Persians, who had taken control when they conquered the Babylonian Empire in 539 B.C.E., ruled the land of Israel. In 333 B.C.E, however, Alexander the Great of Macedonia defeated the Persian army and took control of the entire Middle East. After Alexander's death, his vast empire was divided. The Ptolemaic Dynasty (or simply, the Ptolemies) ruled Egypt. The Seleucid Dynasty ruled Syria and adjacent regions. The land of Israel, located between Egypt and Syria, was originally ruled by the Ptolemies but was later conquered by the Seleucids.

Alexander the Great

During this time, the Jews of Judea enjoyed autonomy over their internal affairs. They were not permitted to conduct foreign policy; they had no army; and they were heavily taxed by foreigners, but there was no interference with dealings among the Jews themselves, and they were permitted to conduct their society in accordance with the laws of the Torah and operate the Temple as they saw fit. The High Priest, who was in charge of the Temple and its service, also supervised matters not directly connected to ritual, such as repair of the city walls and improvement of the aqueducts bringing water to Jerusalem. This, then, was the state of affairs when Judea came under the fateful influence of Hellenism.

Modi'in, the beginning of the Maccabean revolt

-164

-1000   0

The Hellenizers

From the time of Alexander the Great's conquest, all the countries of the Middle East came under the influence of Hellenistic - that is to say Greek - culture (Hellas is Greek for Greece). The peoples of the Middle East tried to imitate the culture of their Greek overlords. Some of these peoples assimilated completely and disappeared as distinct national entities. Greek culture was quite different from the culture of the Jews. The differences were manifest in intellectual fields such as philosophy and literature; in the culture of the body, such as sports and the art of war; and in material culture, such as art, pottery, and architecture.

In Judea, as well, there were those who wished to be part of the Hellenistic culture dominating the entire region. In particular, Jerusalem's upper classes, the wealthy and the priests, who came into close contact with the rulers and were familiar with their customs, began to imitate Greek culture. They began to speak Greek, adopt Greek names, visit the gymnasium where the young athletes wrestled naked, participated in foot races and other sports.

The art of war in Greek culture

Greek culture was idolatrous and contained many elements that were not only foreign but antithetical to the spirit of Jewish tradition. Most Jews remained faithful to the Jewish religion and its customs, and strenuously opposed the foreign culture and the Jews who adopted it.

We can imagine what the conservative Jewish farmers from the small villages of Judea must have thought when they came to Jerusalem and heard - and perhaps even saw - how the High Priest upon completing his service in the Temple would remove his priestly vestments and go to watch athletic contests in the gymnasium.

Those who observed Jewish law saw the Hellenizers as infidels and traitors to all that the nation held holy. The Hellenizers, on the other hand, saw themselves as progressive, as following the spirit of the time; and perceived those who observed Jewish law as fanatics who stood in the way of progress.

Jews oppose the foreign culture

Antiochus IV and his Oppressive Decrees

Antiochus IV

Antiochus IV was a Seleucid monarch who ruled over Syria and the land of Israel; his reign began in the year 175 B.C.E. His policy was different from that of his Hellenistic and Persian predecessors. Until then, the various rulers of the land of Israel had not intervened in religious matters. Antiochus IV, however, wished to consolidate all the peoples under his rule into one homogeneous nation. He therefore prohibited observance of the Jewish commandments and tried by force to compel the Jews to observe Greek customs.

Historical sources describe Antiochus' oppressive measures and the reactions of those who remained faithful to Jewish law.

Moreover, the king sent agents with written orders to Jerusalem and the towns of Judea. Ways and customs foreign to the country were to be introduced. Burnt-offerings, sacrifices, and libations in the Temple were forbidden; Sabbaths and feast-days were to be profaned. Altars, idols, and sacred precincts were to be established; swine and other unclean beasts to be offered in sacrifice. They must leave their sons uncircumcised; they must make themselves in every way abominable, unclean, and profane, and so forget the law and change all their statutes. The penalty for disobedience was death.

(I Maccabees 1:44-50)

-164

-1000   0

Opposition to the Decrees

Hannah mourns her seven dead sons
(From Miszellaneen von MittelRhein)

Some people bowed to Antiochus' decrees, as they had already been influenced by the ways of the Greeks. Many, however, resisted, and there were those willing to sacrifice their lives and the lives of their children in order to keep the commandments of the Torah. The Book of Maccabees tells of women cruelly put to death because they would not agree to leave their sons uncircumcised (I Maccabees 1:60). Particularly well known is the story of Hannah and her seven sons, who were all killed by the Greeks because they refused to worship idols.

According to one of the stories describing those difficult days, Antiochus appointed a governor for Jerusalem named Philippus, and ordered him to require all Jews to bow before an idol of the king (the king himself was also frequently considered a god) and to participate in the sacrifice of a pig. Philippus thought that if he could convince one of the Jewish elders, this would influence the simple people as well. He therefore summoned Elazar, one of the more important priests, and told him to fulfill the king's decree. But Elazar did not agree. Philippus said to him:

"You know that I respect you, and that I wish to make it easy for you. Let us take meat of a kosher animal slaughtered according to your own laws. You will eat before the people, so that they will think that you are eating pork. If you do not agree, I will not be able to violate the king's decree, and I will be compelled to have you put to death.

Elazar replied: "Today, I am ninety years old. If I do as you request, all those younger than I will say, 'Even ninety-year-old Elazar sought to save his life by eating pork. So what do they expect of us?' I would rather die to set an example for my people. Both life and death are in the hands of God, and you must do as you see fit."

When Philippus saw Elazar's stubborn courage, he commanded his men to beat him to death.

(Josippon 14)

55

The Rebellion Begins

How the Jewish rebellion against the Greeks broke out is chronicled in the Book of Maccabees. When a detachment of Greek soldiers arrived at the town of Modi'in to compel its residents to sacrifice a pig to the Greek gods, the officers turned first to Mattathias, scion of the priestly Hasmonean family:

The king's officers who were enforcing apostasy came to the town of Modi'in to see that sacrifice was offered, and many Israelites went over to them. Mattathias and his sons stood in a group. The king's officers spoke to Mattathias: "You are a leader here," they said, "a man of mark and influence in this town, with your sons and brothers at your back. You be the first now to come forward and carry out the king's order. All the nations have done so, as well as the leading men in Judea and the people left in Jerusalem. Then you and your sons will be enrolled among the king's friends; you will all receive high honors, rich rewards of silver and gold, and many further benefits."

To this Mattathias replied in a ringing voice: "Though all the nations within the king's dominions obey him and forsake their ancestral worship, though they have chosen to submit to his commands, yet I and my sons and brothers will follow the Covenant of our fathers. Heaven forbid we should ever abandon the law and its statutes. We will not obey the command of the king, nor will we deviate from our forms of worship."

As soon as he had finished, a Jew stepped forward in full view of all, to offer a sacrifice on the pagan altar at Modi'in, in obedience to the royal decree. The sight stirred Mattathias to indignation; he shook with passion, and in a fury of righteous anger rushed forward and slaughtered the traitor on that very altar. At the same time, he killed the officer sent by the king to enforce sacrifice, and pulled the pagan altar down. . . . "Follow me," he shouted through the town, "every one of you who is zealous for the law and strives to maintain the Covenant!" He and his sons took to the hills, leaving all their belongings behind in the town.

(I Maccabees 2:15-28)

-1000

-164

0

The Marriage of Hannah Daughter of Mattathias

Legend, however, has a different account of the rebellion's outbreak, based on the theme of "droit de seigneur," the right of the first night.

Mattathias calls for revolt by Doré

As part of their campaign to break the spirit of the Jews, the Greeks decreed that every maiden must spend her wedding night in the bed of the regional governor, and that only afterward would she be permitted to her husband. As a result of this decree, the Jews stopped marrying. For three years and three months, no wedding was held in Judea. Then came the time for Hannah, daughter of Mattathias the Hasmonean, to marry. In spite of the decree, Mattathias held a great celebration, inviting the leaders of the nation, for Mattathias' family was extremely prominent. The bride sat, as was customary, at the head table, but suddenly stood up, clapped her hands together, and tore her expensive wedding dress, exposing herself. Everyone looked away in embarrassment, and her brothers ran to fall upon her and kill her for shaming herself and her family.

But Hannah said to them, "Why, when I shame myself before my relatives and friends are you so filled with embarrassment and anger that you wish to kill me, but you agree to surrender me this night so the heathen governor can lie with me? Why do you not learn from Simon and Levy, sons of our forefather Jacob, who avenged the rape of their sister Dinah (Genesis, chapter 34)?"

Everyone realized that Hannah was right; her brothers discussed the matter and came to a decision. They dressed their sister in the finest garments and brought her with great ceremony, at the head of a large procession, to the king. Hannah's brothers declared, "We are the sons of the High Priest, and it is not fitting that our sister be given to the governor. Our sister is fit only for the king himself!" The brothers' words found favor in the king's eyes.

The brothers accompanied Hannah to the royal bedchamber, and thereupon, seized the king and killed him. Afterward, they stormed out, killing ministers, guards, and servants who were in the palace. So began the Hasmonean revolt.

(M. Y. Ben Gurion, miMekor Yisrael 1; Y. D. Eisenstein, Otzar Midrashim: Hannukah)

Fighting for Jerusalem

The Jewish rebels, known also as the Maccabees, were led by Mattathias' son Judah. Antiochus sent out various commanders to defeat the rebels, but it was not an easy war, as the Jews were able to hide in the desert and in mountainous areas where access was difficult for a regular army. Sometimes, the Greek forces managed to defeat the rebels; in many cases, though, it was the Jews who defeated the Greeks in small battles waged in territory difficult for an army's passage and which the Jews knew much better than the foreign forces.

The Jews were well aware of their ultimate objective: Jerusalem and the Temple. They were mourning for both, destroyed by the Greeks.

Jerusalem lay deserted like a wilderness; none of her children went in or out. Her holy place was trampled down; aliens and heathen lodged in her citadel. Joy had been banished from the people of Israel; and the flute and the harp were silent.

(I Maccabees 3:45)

The battle between the Maccabees and the Greeks, by Doré

-164

-1000

0

In place of the joy that had always prevailed at the three annual pilgrimage festivals, Passover, Shavu'ot, and Sukkot, when masses of people went up to Jerusalem, there were now only painful memories. But Judah, Mattathias's son appointed to command the fighters, did not despair. He encouraged the people to fight until they would be able to return to Jerusalem as victors. Before each battle, Judah aroused his soldiers with a short but inspiring message, like his talk before the battle of Emmaus, where, commanding a force of three thousand untrained Jewish fighters without suitable weapons, he defeated five thousand trained, well-armed Greek soldiers:

Judah Maccabee, enamel plaque, France, 16th century

. . . . Judah thus addressed them: "Prepare for action and show yourselves men. Be ready at dawn to fight these heathens who are massed against us to destroy us and our holy place. Better to die fighting than to look on while calamity overwhelms our people and the holy place. And, in any case, whatever Heaven will, is what will come to pass.

(I Maccabees 3:58-60)

1000   2000

The Conquest of Jerusalem and Purification of the Temple

In spite of their inferiority in numbers and armament, after extremely difficult battles throughout Judea, Judah and his men succeeded in capturing Jerusalem. The Jewish victory over the Greeks was a historic instance of the spirit of the fighters being every bit as important as military might. The Book of Maccabees tells of the emotion-filled moment when the Jews returned to Jerusalem as victors, in the year 164 B.C.E., some three years after the rebellion began:

The Purification of the Temple

And Judah and his brothers said: "Now that our enemies have been crushed, let us go up to Jerusalem to cleanse the Temple and rededicate it." So the whole army was assembled and went up to Mount Zion. There they found the Temple laid waste, the altar profaned, the gates burnt down, the courts overgrown like a thicket or wooded hillside, and the priests' rooms in ruin. They tore their garments in mourning, wailed loudly, put ashes on their heads, and fell on their faces.

(I Maccabees 4:36-39)

Judah and his men began cleaning the grounds and restoring the structure. One of their first acts was to erect a new altar in place of the altar that had been desecrated and destroyed by the Greeks.

-1000   -164   0

The Eternal Flame Returns to the Altar

Legend tells that after Judah and his men built the altar and arranged wood on it for a fire, they prepared an animal for sacrifice, laying it upon the altar they had so recently completed. But the holy fire that burned on the altar from the days of Moses and remained miraculously alive in a secret hiding place for the seventy years of Babylonian exile no longer existed, and it was forbidden to use "strange fire." The Maccabees prayed, and in response, fire issued from the stones of the altar and ignited the wood. This same fire continued to burn on the altar until the Temple was finally destroyed by the Romans over two hundred years later.

The altar was dedicated on the twenty-fifth of the Hebrew month of Kislev, three years after it had been desecrated and defiled by the Greeks. To this day, Jews celebrate the twenty-fifth of Kislev as the first night of Hannukah.
(Josippon 18)

The Miracle of the Oil

In the Temple there stood a seven-branched candelabrum known in Hebrew as the Menorah, which burned day and night without interruption. The lights of the Menorah were fueled by olive oil of the finest quality, whose ritual purity was zealously guarded during the entire process of its production. The oil designated for the Menorah was stored in special vessels bearing the seal of the High Priest.

An ancient tradition tells:

When the Greeks entered the Temple, they defiled all the containers of oil, and when the Hasmonean family and their followers prevailed, defeating the Greeks, they searched and found only one container still sealed with the seal of the High Priest. It held enough oil for only one day, but a miracle occurred, and the oil burned for eight days.

The next year they declared the eight days of the miracle to be a holiday for praise and thanksgiving.

(Babylonian Talmud, Shabbat 21b)

An Italian Jew lights the Hanuka Lamp

Hanukkah, the eight days of praise and thanksgiving established over two thousand years ago, continues to be celebrated by Jews the world over to this very day.

-1000

-164

0

Six periods in the history of Israel as reflected in the song "Ma'oz Zur" ("Rock of Ages"), by Miriam Aranne, Israel

By tradition, each night after lighting the Hanukkah candles, we sing the song "Rock of Ages." The words were written by a Jew in thirteenth century Germany whose identity remains unknown. The author did leave us a kind of signature, though. Taken together, the opening letters of the Hebrew verses spell out the author's first name, Mordekhai.

The song describes various moments in history when the Jews were miraculously saved from their oppressors. The second verse describes the Exodus from Egypt; the third verse describes the return from Babylonian exile; the fourth, the Jews' rescue in the time of Mordekhai and Esther, which gave us the Purim festival; and the fifth tells of the Maccabees' victory over the Greeks:

Greeks gathered to attack me in the Hasmonean days; they demolished my towers and polluted all the oils; from the last remaining flask, a miracle was wrought for Israel. Men of wisdom then decreed eight days for hymns of praise.

63

1000

2000

Jerusalem Expands

During the the Hasmonean rule, Jerusalem grew significantly and many new buildings were erected - new residential neighborhoods as well as opulent palaces for members of the upper classes. The Hasmonean rulers themselves lived in a palace near the Temple. New sections were added to the city wall in order to incorporate the new areas that had been built. In the vicinity of the city, outside the wall, wealthy families prepared monumental burial sites, some of which can still be seen today. One the most famous of these is known today as Yad Avshalom or Absalom's tomb; it is named for King David's son Absalom (who lived nearly a millenium earlier). Archaeological excavations in and around Jerusalem have unearthed many remains from the days when the Hasmoneans ruled Jerusalem.

The lower city, part of the reproduction of Jerusalem at the time of the 2nd Temple

GLORY AND DESTRUCTION

GLORY AND DESTRUCTION

Herod and The Hasmonean Dynasty

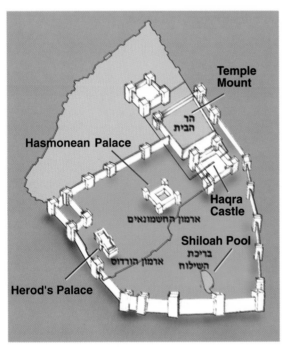

Temple Mount

הר הבית

Hasmonean Palace

Haqra Castle

ארמון החשמונאים

Shiloah Pool

בריכת השילוח ארמון הורדוס

Herod's Palace

Jerusalem in the Hasmonean period
— Wall of the present-day Old City

By struggling against the Greeks, the Jewish people achieved political independence and religious freedom. The rulers of the Hasmonean Dynasty, descendants of Judah the Maccabee and his brothers, expanded Jewish sovereignty over the land of Israel.

The Hasmonean dynasty ruled for roughly a hundred and thirty years, beginning with their conquest of Jerusalem in 164 B.C.E. During this time, the Hasmonean rulers conquered a number of neighboring peoples, including the Idumeans who lived in the southern part of the land of Israel and whom they compelled to convert to Judaism. Ultimately, Hasmonean rule was ended by family feuds and civil wars. The end of Hasmonean rule set the stage for the ascent of Herod, son of an Idumean convert.

In Herod's time, most of the countries surrounding the Mediterranean were ruled by the Roman Empire. Herod, too, although King of Judea, ruled at the behest of the Romans and therefore sought to curry favor with the rulers of Rome by adopting their culture and spreading it throughout his kingdom. Like the Romans, Herod sponsored wrestling matches and chariot races and erected a coliseum for gladiatorial contests. He also erected magnificent edifices throughout his kingdom, as the Romans had in the cities of their empire.

Previous page: The Hippodrome, part of the reproduction of Jerusalem at the 2nd Temple period

Herod Beautifies the Temple and Jerusalem

Herod decided that the Temple in Jerusalem, which had been constructed by the returnees from the Babylonian exile, was not sufficiently impressive. Herod had seen the magnificent temples of Rome and the lands under Roman control and wanted the Temple in Jerusalem to emulate and exceed them in beauty. He also thought that by constructing a larger, more beautiful, Temple he would find favor in the eyes of the Jews and win their loyalty, for he knew that the people saw him as a foreigner and opposed his rule.

When he announced his plan, many, particularly the Rabbis, feared that Herod intended to demolish the Temple and not rebuild it. To calm their fears, Herod first assembled all the materials necessary for the reconstruction, in order to demonstrate his intention to build rather than destroy. Since the most sacred precincts of the Temple could be entered only by the priests, a thousand young priests studied the various crafts required to build the new structure, and they were the ones who carried out the work inside the Temple.

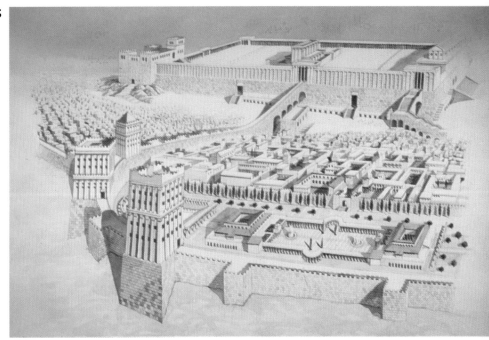

A view of Jerusalem and the Temple in the Herodian Era

The Midrash tells that even after the work of construction had begun, there were still many who remained suspicious of Herod and uncertain the project was worthy. As time went on, however, people noticed that on working days, rain fell only at night, and that during the day, the weather was always mild and favorable to the workers. Thus they concluded that Herod's undertaking had found favor before the Lord.

(Babylonian Talmud, Ta'anit 23a)

1000

2000

Tremendous capital and meticulous planning were invested in rebuilding the Temple; only the finest materials were used. Marble and fine woods were imported from abroad. The Temple itself was significantly enlarged: the courtyard before the Temple, where the pilgrims gathered to celebrate the three annual pilgrimage festivals, was the largest of its kind anywhere in the world at that time.

A sophisticated system of gates, passages, and tunnels was built to accommodate the one hundred thousand and more pilgrims who would come to Jerusalem for the festivals, and augment the city's indigenous population of some one hundred fifty thousand.

The work of construction lasted nine years.

Our Sages declared:

"One who has not seen Herod's edifice has never seen a beautiful building."

(Babylonian Talmud, Baba Batra 4a)

Herod undertook great building projects not only on the Temple Mount, but throughout Jerusalem. He built palaces, an outdoor theater and a hippodrome (an arena for chariot races). He reinforced and expanded the city's walls and constructed gates and towers for fortification. During Herod's reign, Jerusalem was larger and more beautiful than it ever was before or after.

Our Sages said:

"One who has not seen Jerusalem in her glory has never seen a beautiful city."

(Babylonian Talmud, Sukkah 51b)

Interior of a dwelling from the Herodian period
(archaeological finding in the Jewish Quarter)

-1000

20
0

Pilgrimage to Jerusalem

Thousands of Jews from all over the country, as well as the Diaspora, were attracted to make the pilgrimage to Jerusalem and its magnificent Temple. Owing to the efficient measures taken in Jerusalem, the pilgrimage was an edifying experience despite the large number of pilgrims. Our Sages said: "No one ever said, 'There is no room for me to sleep in Jerusalem.'" (Mishnah Avot 5:5). Although the various areas of the Temple teemed with people, no one felt pressed or crowded. It is told that, one Passover, an elderly person was crushed to death. This event was so exceptional that people spoke of it for years after.

Pilgrims on their way to Jerusalem, by A. Halevi

People from all over the country left their homes and fields to go up to the Jerusalem with their families. Various stories are told in this connection.

It was told of a particular man that he forgot to lock his house when he went up to Jerusalem. When he returned, he found a snake coiled on his door knob, such that no one could open the door. In another instance, a man forgot to put his hens back in the hen house before he left for Jerusalem. When he returned, he found several wildcats, that normally prey on chickens, dead in his courtyard: his hens had killed them!

Legends of this type were certainly created to encourage people to fulfill the command to make the pilgrimage to Jerusalem.

The Sages said that Jerusalem does not have impressive natural endowments: her fruits are not as fine as those that grow in the Valley of Genesareth by the Sea of Galilee; nor does Jerusalem have healing springs like those of Tiberias. Why is this so? So that people will not say, "Even if we go up to Jerusalem only to taste her good fruits, it is worthwhile!" Or: "Even if we go up to Jerusalem only to bathe in her healing springs, it is worthwhile." No, the pilgrimage to Jerusalem and the Temple must be for the sole purpose of fulfilling God's commandment.

(Babylonian Talmud, Pesahim 64b and 8b; Jerusalem Talmud, Pe'ah 3:8)

Rebellion and Destruction

After Herod's death, Roman involvement and intervention in everything that went on in Judea increased. The Romans, who ruled a tremendous empire encompassing Europe, North Africa and the Middle East, despised the Jews of Judea. They demanded high taxes, desecrated the Temple, and plundered the Temple's treasures. Every instance of Jewish resistance was cruelly repressed.

Finally, in the year 66 C.E., the Jews of the land of Israel rebelled against the Romans. The rebellion, of course, had not a chance of succeeding. What could a small weak people like the Jews do against the mighty Roman Empire? Nevertheless, Vespasian and Titus, commanders of the Roman army, together with their enormous force of well-trained soldiers, required four full years to put down the rebellion and several more years to finally dispose of all remaining pockets of resistance. In the year 70, after an extended and difficult siege, Jerusalem was conquered and the Temple put to the torch. Massada, the rebels' last stronghold, fell three years later in 73 C.E.

The Second Temple, like the First, was destroyed on the ninth of the Hebrew month of Av. This is the date on which Jews the world over still commemorate the destruction of both Temples, by fasting, special prayers, and other mourning practices.

Hundreds of thousands of Jews were killed during the war against Rome, and tens of thousands were taken as slaves - some to die as gladiators in the arena for the entertainment of the Roman masses, others to serve as domestic slaves in the homes of wealthy Roman citizens, and still others to serve as rowers, chained to their benches in the holds of Roman galleys. The victorious army held a grand victory march in Rome, the commanders and soldiers exhibiting their Jewish captives and the vessels they had plundered from the Temple. To commemorate their victory, the Romans built the Arch of Titus, depicting the subjection of Jews carrying the Temple Menorah into captivity. The arch was first built of wood and stood for twenty years. It was later rebuilt in stone and stands to this day in Rome.

Bas-relief of Roman victors with spoils from the Temple as depicted on the Arch of Titus, Rome

GLORY AND DESTRUCTION

Destruction of the Temple

Yosef ben Matityahu (also known as Josephus Flavius), a Jewish historian who lived at the time, describes the burning of the Second Temple:

As the Temple burned, the Roman soldiers continued to plunder on all sides, and every Jew they met was put to the sword. They took no mercy on the elderly or on children; nor did they make any distinction between those who tried to defend themselves and those who begged for mercy. Groans of the wounded and dying could be heard over the roar of the fire, which destroyed the Temple and everything nearby. It looked as though the entire city of Jerusalem was burning. The noise was awesome: on the one side, the battle cries of the Roman soldiers, and on the other, the agonized screams of the last of the rebel fighters and inhabitants of Jerusalem being slaughtered. Many of the people who had not tasted food for several days summoned the last of their strength to raise their voices in bitter weeping when they saw the Temple going up in flames.

(Yosef ben Matityahu, The Jewish Wars 6)

The Destruction of the Temple by Francisco Hayes, 19th Century (detail)

1000   2000

Why Was the Temple Destroyed?

Our Sages said that the Second Temple was destroyed because of groundless hatred, when Jews hated each other for no reason. Our Sages told various stories of the wickedness of people and their hate for each other. The Babylonian Talmud (Yoma 9b) declares that hatred of one's fellow man is an even graver transgression than the worship of idols. From historical sources, it is clear that factionalism and civil war during the Second Temple period were indeed among the factors that helped the enemies of the Jews to gain control of the country and ultimately destroy it.

There once was a man in Jerusalem who had a friend named Kamtza and an enemy named Bar Kamtza. One day, this man invited his friends to a great banquet and sent his servant to invite his friend, Kamtza. By mistake, the servant invited Bar Kamtza instead. After the banquet had begun, the man noticed Bar Kamtza sitting among his guests: "Why have you come? You hate me. What are you doing in this house? Leave right now!"

But Bar Kamtza replied, "Please do not insult me. Since I am already here, permit me to remain until the end of the banquet."
"No, leave this instant."
But Bar Kamtza replied, "I will pay the price of my meal."
"No!"
"I will pay half the cost of the banquet."
"No!"
"I will pay the entire cost of the banquet."
"No!" and with that, the man took Bar Kamtza by the hand and led him out of the house as all the guests looked on and saw how he humiliated Bar Kamtza.

The Sages said, "Because of Kamtza and Bar Kamtza was Jerusalem destroyed."

(Babylonian Talmud, Gittin 55-56)

-1000

20

0

Why Was the Western Wall Preserved?

Western Wall, Early 20th Century

The Midrash tells that when Jerusalem was conquered, the Romans decided to raze the city to her foundations. The task of destroying the walls surrounding the Temple Mount was divided among certain officers of the Roman army, each one charged with destroying one of the four walls. Three of the officers did precisely as they were commanded, but the officer responsible for destroying the Western Wall left it standing. When asked why he had disobeyed orders, the officer answered, "I did it for the glory of Rome, so that future generations will see what strong walls we had to overcome in order to defeat the Jews."

And the Western Wall still stands.

The Western Wall, Built by the Poor

Legend tells that when Solomon built the First Temple, he divided the work among all the people, officials and officers, priests and Levites, ordinary citizens and the poor. The different tasks - who would make the Holy Ark; who would make the ceremonial curtain; who would make the pillars; and who the walls - were assigned by lot. To the poor fell the task of constructing the Western Wall.

The heads of the different groups collected the money required and employed craftsmen to do the work. Only the poor were unable to raise enough money, and the Western Wall was the only portion of the Temple on which the work did not progress. When the poor people realized this, they themselves went to work: men, women, and children, too, all lent a hand, dug the foundations, transported the stones, raised them to their places, and did not stop working until the wall was completed.

When the Temple was destroyed, only the wall that the poor built by their own labor remained standing.

(Midrash Rabbah, Eikhah 1:32; Ze'ev Vilnay, Agaddot Eretz Yisrael 1)

Memory of the Destruction Lives On in the Hearts of the People

The Jewish people never forgot the destruction of its Temple. Throughout our history, we have commemorated this tragic event in prayer and other practices. The ninth of the Hebrew month of Av, date of the Temple's destruction, is observed each year as a national day of mourning. Here is one example of the many elegies recited on the Ninth of Av. This one is sung by the Sephardi Jews of Jerusalem:

Droplets fall from my eye
For the fall of Jerusalem

I cry night and day
For my brothers who fell

I pour out my soul and lifeblood
To Him who dwells in Heaven

Rock of my Salvation, put anger aside
Arise as a wall to protect us

And let the sun shine
Sevenfold upon us.

Hope for the Redemption and the rebuilding of Jerusalem is also expressed in this poem written in our own time:

In the city of Jerusalem,
Stands a gate of gold.
And an angel of Heaven
Is stationed there

At his post for two thousand years,
Standing there day and night
Until the day
When Jerusalem is redeemed.

(Ya'akov David Kamzon)

"If I forget thee, Jerusalem"
Part of an amulet, Jerusalem, 19th Century

The Eternal Connection Between the Jewish People and Jerusalem

THE ETERNAL CONNECTION BETWEEN THE JEWISH PEOPLE AND JERUSALEM

The People Refuse to Give Up Jerusalem

The Great Jewish Rebellion ended in 70 C.E. with the Temple in ruins and Jerusalem practically devoid of Jews. The destruction, however, did not end the connection between the Jewish people and Jerusalem. Within a short time, the Jews attempted to retake the city by force: after Rome's victory, a new rebellion broke out under the leadership of the charismatic Simon, son of Koziba, remembered by the epithet "Bar Kokhba" - Hebrew for "son of a star."

For three years, from 132 to 135 C.E., battles raged between Bar Kokhba's men and the armies of Rome. The Jews of neighboring countries ruled by the Romans also supported this rebellion. Over the course of the war, Bar Kokhba actually gained control of Jerusalem for a short period, sufficient to mint coins with Jewish symbols, which he dated from "the Redemption of Israel" and "the Liberation of Jerusalem." But the Romans sent a powerful army to the land of Israel and within three years managed to suppress the rebellion. They first captured the Galilee - the northern part of the country - and later Jerusalem. Betar, a small town near Jerusalem that served as the rebels' last fortification, fell to the Romans. Bar Kokhba himself was killed at Betar.

A cave used in the Bar Kokhba Rebellion
(reconstruction)

The facade of the
Holy Temple on a coin
minted by Bar Kokhba
at the time of the first
rebellion

Jews mourning the Destruction of the Temple and Jerusalem on the Ninth of Av

According to tradition, Betar's destruction also fell on the ninth of the Hebrew month of Av, as did the destruction of the two Temples before it.

After the Bar Kokhba Revolt, the Romans rebuilt Jerusalem as a pagan city, renaming it Aelia Capitolina. Entry was forbidden to Jews, with the exception of the Ninth of Av when they were permitted to visit Jerusalem and mourn the destruction of their land, their city, and their Temple.

From this time onward, Jews have maintained their ties with Jerusalem in different ways - the primary one being prayer, in which they remember Jerusalem on both weekdays and festivals.

1800

1000

2000

The People Preserve the Memory of Jerusalem

Have mercy, Lord our God,
on Israel Your people,
on Jerusalem Your city,
on Zion the abode of Your Majesty,
on the royal house of David, Your chosen one,
and on the great and holy Temple
that bears Your name.

(Grace After Meals, Ashkenazi Rite)

Dwell in Jerusalem, Your city,
as You have promised,
and speedily establish there the throne
of David Your servant,
and rebuild it as an everlasting structure,
speedily in our days.
Blessed are You, O God, builder of Jerusalem.

(Weekday Amidah, Sephardi Rite)

"רַחֵם נָא ה' אֱ-לוֹהֵינוּ
עַל יִשְׂרָאֵל עַמֶּךָ
וְעַל יְרוּשָׁלַיִם עִירֶךָ
וְעַל צִיּוֹן מִשְׁכַּן כְּבוֹדֶךָ
וְעַל מַלְכוּת בֵּית דָּוִד מְשִׁיחֶךָ
וְעַל הַבַּיִת הַגָּדוֹל וְהַקָּדוֹשׁ
שֶׁנִּקְרָא שִׁמְךָ עָלָיו."

"תִּשְׁכּוֹן בְּתוֹךְ יְרוּשָׁלַיִם
עִירְךָ כַּאֲשֶׁר דִּבַּרְתָּ,
וְכִסֵּא דָוִד עַבְדְּךָ מְהֵרָה בְּתוֹכָהּ תָּכִין,
וּבְנֵה אוֹתָהּ בִּנְיַן עוֹלָם בִּמְהֵרָה בְיָמֵינוּ.
בָּרוּךְ אַתָּה ה', בּוֹנֵה יְרוּשָׁלָיִם."

-1000   0   70

A folk story relates that not only do the Jewish people mourn for the Temple but that the Temple also mourns for the Jewish people. It is told that each year on the night of the Ninth of Av, a sigh and a moan can be heard to emerge from the Western Wall.

M. M. Biderman, Serid Mikdashenu (Remnant of Our Temple)

In various Jewish communities, it is customary to print the booklets used for the prayers of mourning recited on the Ninth of Av on inexpensive paper with simple binding. This custom expresses the faith that the redemption will come speedily, and that it would therefore be a waste to invest in producing a fine edition of these prayers, since soon there will be no need for them. . . .

During Napoleon's campaign against Russia, as he passed through a small Jewish shtetl, he expressed a desire to see the inside of a synagogue. By chance it was the fast of the Ninth of Av, and the Jews were sitting in darkness on the floor weeping as they prayed. When it was explained to Napoleon that the reason for the weeping was for the destruction of the Temple, he asked, "When did this happen?"

"Two thousand years ago," he was told.

Upon hearing this, the Emperor declared, "A people who knows how to remember its land for two thousand years, will certainly find the way to return."

(Folk story told by the Jews of Russia; Dov Noy, Golah veEretz Yisrael)

1800

1000

2000

Jerusalem in the hands of Christians and Muslims

In the many generations that have passed since Bar Kokhba and his rebels fell defeated, powerful empires have risen and fallen. While most Jews were living in the lands of the Diaspora, various peoples ruled the land of Israel for long periods: the Byzantine Christians, heirs of Rome; the Moslems, who came from the Arabian Peninsula in the seventh century and conquered the entire Middle East and much more; the Crusaders, who hailed from Europe; the Mamelukes from Egypt; and the Ottomans from the center of their Empire in Istanbul, Turkey. Each conquest left an indelible impression upon the city, strengthening the connection between Jerusalem and Islam, on the one hand, and Jerusalem and Christianity on the other. Thus today, Jerusalem is home to tens of churches and mosques.

Jerusalem and the Diaspora

Throughout these periods, depending on the political, religious, and economic situation, the Jewish community of Palestine knew good fortune and bad. There were times when Jerusalem was a well organized community of scholars, yeshivot, and communal institutions; and there were other times, when barely a single Jew lived in Jerusalem. No matter what their situation in Jerusalem and the Diaspora, however, the Jews never forgot their capital and the site of their ancient Temple. The moment circumstances changed for the better, there were always Jews who came from near and far to make Jerusalem their home.

At the Western Wall, you could always meet Jews from all over the Diaspora: Sepharadim and Ashkenazim, Jews from North Africa, the Middle East, and Yemen. Their clothing and language might be different, but their prayer and its content were the same: they prayed in Hebrew for the restoration of Jerusalem.

The aspiration to "go up" to Jerusalem, together with the practical difficulty of realizing this dream, created an imaginary reality, which testified to the deep emotional connection between the Diaspora Jew and his or her beloved Jerusalem. There was a widespread legend that an underground tunnel, through which it was possible to pass in a very short time, connected the Diaspora to the land of Israel. According to the legend, there was no doubt of the tunnel's existence; its entrance, however, was all but impossible to find. It is told of different scholars, including Rabbi Shalom Shabbazi of Yemen and Rabbi Joseph Chaim of Baghdad, that they would disappear from their homes on Friday and spend the Sabbath in Jerusalem, returning home only on Saturday night.

THE ETERNAL CONNECTION BETWEEN THE JEWISH PEOPLE AND JERUSALEM

A particular old man was sick, and his doctors said that he must drink goat's milk. The man purchased a goat, but one day, without warning, she disappeared. A few days later she returned, her udders filled with milk that had the flavor of paradise. The goat would repeat this strange behavior from time to time until the old man said to his son, "I want to know where the goat is disappearing."

The son tied a rope to the goat's tail, and when she began to wander, he held on to the rope and followed. They entered a cave, and after a long time, they emerged in a fertile country flowing with milk and honey. When the son asked people where he was, they told him, "You are in the land of Israel."

The son penned a note telling his father what had happened. He wrote that his father should join him in the land of Israel by following the goat through the cave as he had. The son fastened the note to the goat's ear, and she returned home by herself. When the old man saw the goat returning without his son, he was certain that his son had been killed. Realizing that the sight of the goat would always bring him painful memories of his dead son, the man slaughtered her. Only afterward did he discover the note attached to the goat's ear. But what was done was done. The goat was dead, and the underground route to the Holy Land would remain forever secret.

(Adapted from Shemu'el Yosef Agnon, "The Story of the Goat")

1000

1800

2000

*G*uests in Jerusalem

Along with connections to Jerusalem expressed in legend, there were tangible links of various types. Travelers from countries of the Diaspora visited the Holy Land. Pilgrims visited the holy places, particularly Jerusalem. During most periods, people also immigrated from many countries, settled in the city, and strengthened the indigenous Jewish community.

Rabbi Moshe son of Maimon, Maimonides, the greatest Jewish sage and scholar of the Middle Ages, visited Israel in the twelfth century on his way from Morocco to Egypt.

He wrote: . . . We left Acre [on the Mediterranean coast of Palestine] to make the dangerous trip to Jerusalem, and I entered the site of the great and holy Temple and prayed there on Sunday. On the ninth of [the Hebrew month] Heshvan, I left Jerusalem for Hebron to kiss the graves of my forefathers [Abraham, Isaac, and Jacob] at the Cave of Makhpelah. I took a vow that these two days [when I visited Jerusalem and Hebron] would be for me as festivals devoted to prayer and rejoicing. . . . As I was granted to pray in the Holy Land in its destruction, so may I and the entire Jewish people be granted to see her speedily comforted, amen.

(R. Eliezer Azkari, Sefer Haredim)

A bronze statue of Maimonides by Amadeo Olmo, 1964, located in Cordoba, Spain, where Maimonides was born

In the middle of the sixteenth century, the sage, Rabbi Zekhariah Ildahari of Yemen toured the Holy Land. He visited the different cities, and later wrote in rhymed Hebrew of his visit to Jerusalem. He described how he went around the ruins of the city and prayed for her restoration. Here is his description of an encounter with other Jews he happened to meet on the Mount of Olives:

"... And I saw a group of people - adults, children, and old people - under a tree on the Mount of Olives. And I arose and approached them to see who they were." When Rabbi Zekhariah saw that after they finished eating and drinking, the members of the group went back to reciting psalms and elegies, he turned to them and said: *"... Prepare yourselves for the speedy restoration of His house, for it is imminent. We will soon receive the good tidings of our salvation and Redemption. And as you have drunk on His holy mountain, and wept for the destruction of His Temple, so shall you drink to its reconstruction, when it again stands in its place.*

(Rabbi Zekhariah Ildahari, Sefer haMusar, Chapter 22)

Going Up to Jerusalem from the Ends of the Diaspora

Others came to settle in Jerusalem. The medieval poet, Yehudah Halevi, wrote in his philosophical work, The Kuzari, of the importance of the land of Israel to the Jewish people and of the obligation to settle here. In his poems, he wrote constantly of Jerusalem.

O beautiful one, joy of the universe, city of the great King,

For you, my soul has longed from the furthest corner of the West.

My heart is in the East, and I am at the farthest end of the West,

How can I taste, how can anything in life be sweet?

1000

1800

2000

In the year 1140, Rabbi Yehuda Halevi went up to the Holy Land. According to tradition, when he arrived at the gates of Jerusalem, he tore his clothing and recited an elegy which he himself had composed: "O Zion, will you not ask after your captive sons?" At that moment an Islamic zealot passed by on horseback. The man became enraged at seeing a Jew immersed in fervent prayer and trampled Rabbi Yehuda Halevi to death with his horse.

In the book of Numbers (33:53), we find:

"And you shall dwell in the land, for unto you have I given the land to possess it."

On this verse, Nahmanides writes, "In my opinion, this is a positive obligation. The Jewish people is commanded to dwell in the land of Israel and possess it."

-1000   0   70

The Nahmanides Synagogue in the Old City of Jerusalem

As Yehuda Halevi had before him, Nahmanides, foremost Jewish authority in the generation after Maimonides, also left Spain for the land of Israel. When Nahmanides arrived in Jerusalem in 1267, he found some two thousand residents, only two of whom were Jewish, brothers, who supported themselves as dyers of textiles; Nahmanides was a guest in their home.

He stayed with them a month. On Rosh HaShanah, he gave a sermon on repentance to a small congregation of Jews, who had gathered from all over the country; the words of his sermon virtually dripped with gall. He had abandoned his home - his rabbinic court, he said. At the gate of the Jewish quarter of Gerona, he had taken leave of his beloved friends, and come to see the Temple, to see its remains. To see and to weep for it. . . . But what had he found here? Two Jewish dyers and nothing else. (Zvi Barmeir)

Nahmanides, however, did not remain depressed for long. He turned energetically to improving the situation. In a letter to his family in Spain, Nahmanides related: "We urged them to act, and among the ruins, they found a house built of marble pillars with a lovely dome. We began using it for a synagogue, for the city is open, and anyone who wishes can acquire a ruined building by simply making use of it. They volunteered to repair the house, and they have already begun refurbishing it. Then they sent to Nablus for the Torah scrolls that were originally in Jerusalem."

Even as he wrote to his family in distant Spain, Nahmanides took heart. His first efforts had already borne fruit; clearly, the situation in Jerusalem was improving. He sang to himself a melody sung by the Jews of his native Gerona.

O, Jerusalem
Honored city!
Whose fame is known
Throughout the world
We will yet see her
Standing on her mountain, rebuilt.

(Moshe Atias, Romancero Sefaradi)

1000

1800

2000

Rabbi Yehudah heHasid, who came to Jerusalem from Poland in 1700, was unique among immigrants to the Holy Land. Frequently fasting and praying for the salvation of Israel, he travelled from place to place among the communities of Europe, inspiring Jews with his sermons, calling them to repent in order to bring the Redemption. His impressive figure, clad all in white and his pleasing voice, aroused his audiences to great fervor. Sometimes, so that his words would make an even greater impression, he would deliver his sermon while holding a Torah scroll in his arms. From time to time, he would go upstairs to the women's section and speak directly to the women - an extremely unusual practice, which always created a great sensation. Rabbi Yehudah heHasid believed that the Redemption was near, and that therefore the time was ripe to emigrate to the land of Israel: many were persuaded.

He organized a group of some fifteen hundred persons, and they left for the long and harrowing journey to the Holy Land. A large number died along the way from exhaustion and disease; some returned home. No more than eight hundred finally arrived in Jerusalem. Upon his arrival, Rabbi Yehudah heHasid instructed his followers to purchase land for a synagogue. A few days later, Rabbi Yehudah heHasid suddenly died. His congregation was left without teacher or leader. His followers were thrown into mental and economic distress and many were compelled to return to the Diaspora.

The land his followers acquired did indeed become the site of a great synagogue. Its ruins, with one arch restored, can still be seen in Jerusalem's Jewish Quarter; it is known as Hurvat Rabbi Yehudah heHasid.

The Hurvah Synagogue:

In its glory

Destroyed by the Jordanians

As it appears today, partially reconstructed

-1000

0

70

Torah Scholars in Jerusalem

As the Jewish population of Jerusalem grew, there was a great increase in the number of yeshivot, and Jerusalem became a center for Torah study, drawing renowned rabbis from all over the Diaspora.

Rabbi Shalom Sharabi was a rabbi who lived in Yemen in the seventeenth century. He had extensive command of the entire literature of Torah and excelled particularly in the secrets of Jewish mysticism - the Kabbalah. Rabbi Shalom arrived in Jerusalem with no worldly goods. He wanted to continue his studies, and turned to Yeshivat Beit El, a center for the study of Kabbalah in Jerusalem. All who studied there were accomplished scholars, and Rabbi Shalom, who was still very young, did not dare request acceptance among them. He therefore asked Rabbi Gedalyah Hayyun, head of the yeshiva, to employ him as caretaker. In fact, there was little work for a caretaker; nevertheless, Rabbi Gedalyah agreed. Rabbi Shalom waited on the scholars, serving them coffee and listening to their discussions. He quickly realized that his knowledge of the Kabbalah far exceeded theirs. Sometimes questions would arise in the yeshiva. The young Rabbi Shalom always knew the answers. When the scholars would go home at night, R. Shalom would write the answers on a slip of paper and leave it in the study hall.

Rabbi Hayyun investigated and, after a time, discovered that it was Rabbi Shalom who was writing the answers. From that time on, Rabbi Shalom Sharabi became a full member of the yeshiva, and when Rabbi Gedalyah Hiyyun died, Rabbi Shalom took over as head of the yeshiva.

(Malkah Eli-Pudiel, BeSa'arot Teiman; Re'uven Nana, Otzar haMa'asiyot)

Every night, Rabbi Shalom Sharabi would sit and meditate on the Kabbalah, and the prophet Elijah would appear to study with him. No one knew of this secret except the woman who cleaned the yeshiva at night. Rabbi Sharabi asked her not to reveal the secret to anyone. Each night she would bring two glasses of water, one for the rabbi and one for Elijah. As her reward for maintaining the secret, the rabbi promised that she would also have a place in his yeshiva in the world to come. Before her death, the woman requested to be buried close to the grave of the rabbi, in order to remind him of his promise.

(S. Z. Cahane, Yerushalayim haAtikah)

1000   1800   2000

At approximately the same time, Rabbi Hayyim ibn Atar, another great scholar, arrived in Jerusalem from Morocco. In Or haHayyim, his commentary on the Torah, Rabbi Hayyim ibn Atar writes, "The only source of joy is living in the land of Israel." It was on this basis that he decided: "I saw no choice but to arise and go up to the place that was always on my mind, the place where God's presence dwells, the exalted, beloved city" - Jerusalem.
(Or haHayyim on Deuteronomy 26:1; and Introduction to Or haHayyim).

Once in Jerusalem, he opened a yeshiva, where none but the most outstanding scholars studied.

R. Hayyim ibn Atar's name became famous far beyond the land of Israel. Even in Eastern Europe, his greatness was renowned. This was the time of Rabbi Yisrael Ba'al Shem Tov, founder of the Hasidic movement. The Hasidim tell that Rabbi Yisrael wished to go up to Jerusalem to meet Rabbi Hayyim ibn Atar, because he believed that if the two of them would meet at the Western Wall, the final Redemption was certain to come.

Unfortunately, it seems that the time was not ripe for their meeting:

Legend tells: When Rabbi Yisrael Ba'al Shem Tov journeyed to the land of Israel, he confronted various obstacles. Brigands attacked him; severe storms raged. In one storm, R. Yisrael's daughter, Idel, was cast into the sea and miraculously saved. But R. Yisrael understood that his journey was not desired by Heaven, and he returned to his own country. When he arrived there, he learned that in the meantime, Rabbi Hayyim ibn Atar had died. Rabbi Yisrael's dream of bringing the Redemption had to be put aside for the time being.

(Gedalyah Nig'al, haSiferut haHasidit; Martin Buber, Tales of the Hasidim)

The Synagogue of R. Hayyim ibn Atar
in the Old City of Jerusalem

GROWTH AND DEVELOPMENT -
JERUSALEM IN THE MODERN PERIOD

Jerusalem in the First Half of the Nineteenth Century

For centuries following the destruction of the Temple, Jerusalem was little more than a village with a small and needy Jewish community. A hundred and fifty years ago, Jerusalem's population numbered about twelve thousand, half of whom were Jews. In that period, the land of Israel was part of the Ottoman Empire, ruled by the Turks, whose administrative practices lagged greatly behind those of European countries. Modern innovations long accepted in Europe, such as transportation, mail, plumbing, and street lights reached the land of Israel very slowly.

Transportation such as there is in our day did not exist. Near the Jaffa Gate of the Old City, you could always find a group of drivers and a rank of fine-looking wagons. For the price of one metelik [a Turkish coin, the equivalent of a penny], you could ride to Abu Batzal at the end of Jaffa Road. . . . It was difficult for a young woman to ride in a wagon, though, since most of the drivers were Arabs. All the girls were afraid to get into a wagon alone, and before boarding, they would wait for a man in whose company they could ride. The driver, impatient with waiting, would become angry and direct all sorts of curses at any young lady who waited for a male passenger. One time, I saw an Orthodox Jew sitting in a wagon, and I was sure everything would be all right, so I also climbed in and paid the driver. Just as the horses were about to move, the Jew jumped off the wagon as though bitten by a snake, as he did not wish to ride together with a woman. Poor me! I had to sit there in fear all the way home. When I got there, I was as white as a sheet.

(Rivka Duvshani, Pirkei Yoman Hayyim)

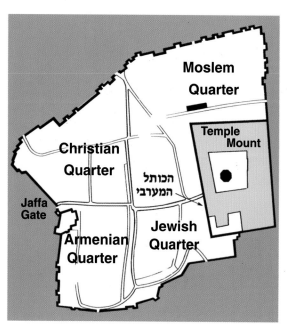

The Old City of Jerusalem

Previous page: Mishkenot Sha'ananim, by S. Manning, 1873

-1000   0

Wagons awaiting passengers at the Jaffa Gate

Many of the city's Jews were elderly people who had left their homes abroad because being buried in the land of Israel was considered a great merit. These people lived on money sent by their children who remained in the Diaspora, or on charity sent by their home communities.

1800   1900
1000   2000

Aunt Delicia immigrated to the land of Israel from Salonika in her old age. Every month, her children sent her several gold Napoleons by Turkish mail, and from this money she would pay her meager expenses and give charity to the synagogue, the soup kitchen, the poor, the cantor, and the beadle. Once, when her money did not arrive on time and she was unable to donate the funds she had promised to charity, Aunt Delicia was extremely embarrassed and quite at her wits' end.

Aunt Delicia lived in the same apartment as an elderly couple with whom she shared a hallway. One day, she noticed the husband taking money from his talit bag, so when the neighbors were not home, she entered their section of the apartment and took one gold Napoleon from the talit bag, intending to return it when the mail came. When the beadle came to collect money for the different institutions, she happily gave him the coin she had taken, feeling that her honor had been restored. She hoped that her money would arrive before her elderly neighbors became aware that a coin was missing. Fortune, however, was not with her; her neighbor counted his money that same night and discovered his loss.

The elderly couple's suspicion of course fell upon Aunt Delicia, who, after all, lived in the same apartment. They took their suspicions to the rabbi, who immediately summoned her.

Aunt Delicia admitted her guilt without hesitation but claimed, "I did not steal. I only borrowed the money, and I will return it as soon as money arrives from my children."

The rabbi replied: "How do I know you are telling the truth? I must investigate. I will give you a glass of extremely bitter water. You must drink it, and if you are lying, your stomach will swell." Aunt Delicia replied, "I am not lying, and I am prepared to do anything the rabbi says." The rabbi went for a glass of water from the kitchen and secretly told his wife to add two teaspoons of honey. Aunt Delicia drank the water quickly, and when she finished she said, "Didn't I tell you I took the money with intention to return it? See, my stomach has not become swollen, and although the honorable rabbi said that the water was bitter, to me it tasted sweet."

Shortly thereafter, her money arrived by mail, and Aunt Delicia returned the gold Napoleon to her neighbors.

(Sha'ul Angel-Malakhi, Sha'alu Shelom Yerushalayim)

-1000

0

Most of Jerusalem's residents were almost penniless and barely survived on the money they received from abroad or on the income they earned from various trades that could hardly support those who engaged in them. Most lived under the extremely difficult conditions. Whole families lived in one small room, with one toilet in the courtyard. The little money they had never sufficed for clothing and not always for food.

Next to the four synagogues of the Sephardi community, to which you descend ten cubits from the street, are located a number of courtyards, to which you must also go down several stairs. In these structures live the poorest of families, each family in one room. The rooms are actually cellars dug into the earth; their interiors are completely dark - they haven't the least crack of a window. The floors are damp earth; the walls - unplastered stones, old, hollow, and covered with dust. On the floor, worn out sheets slippery from dirt are spread out on mats.

(Yehudah Burla, Alilot Akavyah)

Such were the conditions under which most of Jerusalem's residents lived, with hunger and disease taking a tremendous toll and claiming their victims particularly among the infants, but among the adult population as well.

A typical alley way in the Jewish Quarter, Ottoman Period

1000   1800   1900   2000

Moses Montefiore, the Knight who Loved Jerusalem

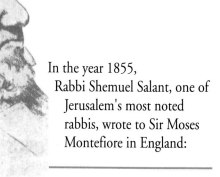

Sir Moses Montefiore was born into an Italian Jewish family, but it was in England, where he held various important positions, that he became wealthy and famous and received the title of "knight." At the age of thirty-nine, having amassed a large fortune in banking and securities, Montefiore decided to dedicate all his time to communal work and helping Jews throughout the world. He traveled to distant lands, such as Syria, Russia, Morocco, and Romania, to intercede with kings and ministers on behalf of his fellow Jews and continued this activity for many years. He died at the age of one hundred and one.

Sir Moses Montefiore felt a particularly strong connection to Jerusalem and had the name of the holy city inscribed on his family coat of arms. He visited there seven times, the last time when he was ninety.

Near the end of the nineteenth century, many people thought that the only way to improve the lot of Jerusalem's poor was to remove them from the crowding of the Old City and build decent modern housing for them, outside the city walls.

In the year 1855, Rabbi Shemuel Salant, one of Jerusalem's most noted rabbis, wrote to Sir Moses Montefiore in England:

To our Good Friend,
the Beloved Sir Moses Montefiore,

Your brothers who live in Jerusalem are poor. They do not have money to purchase land outside the city walls. Help us, honorable sir, to settle outside the walls of Jerusalem, so that many more of our brothers can come to live in our holy city.

Rabbi Shemuel Salant,
The holy city of Jerusalem

The Montefiore family crest

-1000   0

Mishkenot Sha'ananim
the 1st neighborhood built outside the walls (1855)

Sir Moses helped establish a new neighborhood in Jerusalem named Mishkenot Sha'ananim, the first Jewish neighborhood built outside the city walls.

In those days, the building of the Montefiore neighborhood began: several houses were built near the railway station, and people started moving there. They were afraid, however, because they thought there was greater security from attack and theft inside [the city walls], while who knew what might happen outside? Yet, as time went on, people saw it was better: that there was more light and air, and that the houses were pleasant with large rooms. . . . Slowly, but surely, new neighborhoods rose up, and people began leaving the Old City. Each person [who consented to live in Mishkenot Sha'ananim] was given an apartment free for three years, and that is how people were attracted to move outside the walls.

(Rivka Duvshani, Pirkei Yoman Hayyim)

Another project undertaken by Moses Montefiore on behalf of Jerusalem's Jews was the construction of a wind-driven flour mill in the Yemin Moshe neighborhood. His idea was to use modern methods to produce high grade flour cheaply, and thus provide income for Jerusalem's poor. When the windmill was finally completed, owners of older, more primitive flour mills were afraid they would lose their livelihood, and they commissioned a sorcerer to place a curse on the windmill, so that it would not work. The mill worked for many years, however, in spite of the curse. When some years later it broke down, steam-powered mills had already been introduced, so there was no reason to repair it, but Montefiore's windmill is still a landmark and can be seen not far from downtown Jerusalem.

Jerusalem's poor were so taken with the wealthy, important Montefiore and his magnificent coach, the like of which Jerusalem had never seen, that they told all sorts of wonderful stories about Montefiore and his legendary wealth.

1000   1800   1900   2000

Montefiore's coach

When Montefiore was received by the Czar of Russia, he wore a suit decorated with diamonds and ten buttons of pure gold. The cost of each button was 5,000 rubles. . . .

Montefiore had a wondrous coach, which he had built especially for his trips to the many countries he visited. It had room for the kosher food he took with him, and for a Torah scroll. When it snowed, the wheels could be removed and the coach converted to a sled (!) After Montefiore's death, his coach was brought to Jerusalem.

(N. Ausubel, A Treasury of Jewish Folklore; Ari Ibn-Zahav, Shishim Shanah veShanah)

It is told that Rabbi Shemuel Salant journeyed to England and visited the palace of Sir Moses Montefiore. Montefiore showed him the many rooms, his drawing room, the bedrooms, the kitchen, and the library. In each room, the guest from Jerusalem's reaction was the same: "I have better."

When Montefiore visited Jerusalem, he was extremely curious to see Rabbi Salant's "palace," but when he arrived at the rabbi's apartment, he saw that it had but one room. Montefiore asked: "Why did you say that you have better?" Rabbi Salant replied: "Look, Sir Moses, here I have my lounge, my bedroom, my kitchen, and my library. I never have to run from room to room."

-1000

0

New Neighborhoods in Jerusalem

Following construction of Mishkenot Sha'ananim, additional Jewish neighborhoods were built outside the walls of Jerusalem: some by the residents of the Old City, some by new immigrants, and some by philanthropists. The first group of Jerusalemites to build a neighborhood for themselves outside the walls was one of the poorest communities in the city, Jews who hailed from Morocco, who named their neighborhood Mahaneh Yisrael.

The need for new residential neighborhoods continued to be an acute problem. With the establishment of these new neighborhoods, health and sanitation in Jerusalem began to improve, infant mortality diminished, and the Jewish community of Jerusalem grew. At the same time, immigration from the Diaspora was on the rise. There had always been immigration to Jerusalem, but for various reasons the number of immigrants increased noticeably at the end of the nineteenth century. Jews came from Morocco, the Balkans, Eastern Europe, Persia, and Yemen - all of them needing homes. Some of the Yemenite immigrants, who were extremely poor, could not find housing within Jerusalem and settled in the neighboring Arab village of Silwan. But some of the immigrants were people of means.

An early neighborhood outside the walls

We are the pioneers,
Vanguard of all generations
A living wall, will we build around you,
O Jerusalem;
We clear your rubble and set your cornerstones.
Bread and water is all we ask.

And we build stone upon stone, row upon row,
A house arises, then another, a row, street,
a district.
Though we build with our blood,
Our hearts swell with pride
Every empty space - a row of houses, a great city,
A dwelling for the Holy Spirit.

(Ari Ibn-Zahav, Yerushalayim Shel Ma'alah)

97

1800   1900
                2000
1000

The Pioneering Immigrants and Their Work in Jerusalem

With Each Stone

With the scattered stones,
Let me fill your crevices;
Strengthen me with your hammers.
Perhaps I appease my homeland and atone the sin
Of the nation that did not rebuild its ruins

How good to know I am a stone
As all others in Jerusalem
How great my joy to be united with the wall
But my soul was always with my people,
In good times and bad,
Why do I lack the power for action that my soul
does crave

So take me with the Jerusalem limestone and
Place me in your walls
Cover me with plaster,
And from the wall will my bones rejoice
As they yearn for the Messiah

(Yehuda Qarni)

Theodore Herzl founded the Zionist Movement in 1897. Herzl aimed to convince not only the Jews, but world political leaders too, of the importance of the Jews' return to the land of Israel. In 1898, when the German Kaiser, Wilhelm II, visited Jerusalem, Herzl traveled to meet with him.

In 1881, following violent pogroms, hundreds of thousands of Jews left Russia for different countries, particularly the United States. A small number of emigrants, however, turned to the land of Israel. These Jews were entirely different from those already living here. These new immigrants were young men and women without families, influenced by the new nationalist ideologies, who came to the land of Israel believing in the Jewish people's return to its ancient homeland. Most of them held modern ideas fashionable at that time in Europe and did not observe the religious precepts. They called themselves pioneers, because they saw themselves as the vanguard after whom all Jews would follow. These pioneers laid the foundation for such institutions of modern culture in Jerusalem as Hebrew newspapers, a Jewish museum, and modern Hebrew education. They were also the ones who, following the lead of a Hebrew philologist named Eliezer Ben Yehudah, adopted Hebrew as their spoken language.

In 1881, Eliezer Ben Yehudah moved to Jerusalem, where he worked to fulfill his dream of restoring Hebrew as the spoken language of the Jews. Until then, Hebrew had served almost exclusively as the language of prayer and study of holy texts. Here and there, rabbis from different parts of the world communicated to each other in Hebrew, but Hebrew did not serve as the language of the home or street, nor was it any child's mother tongue. Eliezer Ben Yehudah and his wife Devorah spoke only Hebrew in their home, and their son, Itamar, who was born in 1882, is considered the first child in the modern period to grow up speaking Hebrew. Ben Yehudah tried to speak Hebrew with other people as well; this was not always easy, even when the other person was well versed in written Hebrew.

Eliezer Ben-Yehudah campaigning for the Hebrew language

Eliezer Ben Yehudah once met Rabbi Shemuel Mohilever, one of the most important rabbis in Russia and an active member of the Zionist Movement. Ben Yehudah spoke Hebrew. Rabbi Mohilever found it difficult to follow Ben Yehudah's fluent speech, and when the rabbi tried to respond in Hebrew, he found he could not, as he was accustomed only to reading the language. Ben Yehuda continued speaking Hebrew, and in the end, Rabbi Mohilever said to him, "Young man, don't be a fool; speak like a normal human being!"

(M. Lipson, miDor Dor)

Boris Schatz was a sculptor, who came to Jerusalem in 1906, hoping to establish an art museum. Several years earlier, he had met Theodore Herzl and spoken with him about establishing a school and museum of Jewish art in Jerusalem:

When I finished speaking, I waited, my heart pounding. What would he say to the idea?
"Fine, we'll do it," he whispered. And after a short pause, he asked, "And what will you call your school?"
"Bezalel," I answered, "Bezalel, the first Jewish artist,
who built the Temple in the desert so long ago."
"Temple in the desert," Herzl repeated mechanically as his beautiful, sad eyes stared at some distant, infinite horizon. . . .

(Ariella Har'el, Mikdash baMidbar [Temple in the Desert])

The Bezalel School has since trained thousands of young Israeli artists, and its art collection laid the foundation for the Israel Museum in Jerusalem.

The Bezalel Academy - Jerusalem's first art academy

Art work from Bezalel

THE BRITISH MANDATE

orld War I

The period of Jewish growth and development in Jerusalem came to a sudden halt in 1914 with the outbreak of World War I. In this war, Britain, France, and Russia were allied, against the Turkish, Ottoman Empire - which controlled the land of Israel - and Germany. The British army invaded the land of Israel from Egypt in the south; the weaker Turkish army retreated steadily northward.

The situation in Israel in general, and in Jerusalem in particular, was appalling. The Turkish authorities were totally preoccupied with supplying their army, and civilians, particularly the city dwellers, suffered from a dire shortage of food. Many Jews who subsisted on money sent from abroad were left without any income when the war disrupted the mails and communications between banks. People sold their most valuable household possessions to Arabs from the nearby villages for a little wheat or a few vegetables.

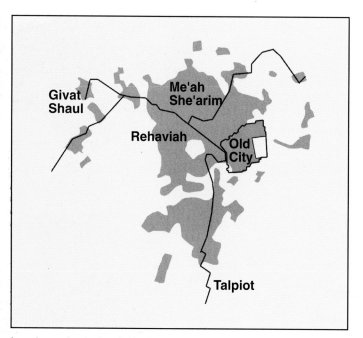

Jerusalem under the British Mandate © Martin Gilbert, 1977

A milkman in old Jerusalem

-1000   0

The shortage finally struck home as the house began to empty. The beautiful wooden chests that adorned the house gradually lost their radiance for me as all the wonders they held slowly disappeared. The cupboards themselves were finally removed one at a time, and every corner of the house that was exposed revealed barrenness and great despair. The expensive cupboard - hand carved and painted bright brown - that stood on round, ornamental legs was also put up for sale. Inside, we always kept our Passover dishes, a lovely set of porcelain and glass dishes, with gold-embroidered table cloths. Nothing remained except the bare minimum we needed to get by. The house appeared as though thieves had broken in and taken everything.

(Ezra Hamenahem, Sippurei haIr haAtikah)

People fell upon the little bit of food sent by Jews from America to help the distressed population of Jerusalem and fought over cans of sardines and jars of jam. Their clothes became shabby, and they began wearing their Sabbath clothes on weekdays, until these too wore out and they were forced to go about in rags. Some wore clothes that arrived in packages from America and caused great laughter, because they looked so strange to the Jews of the city. One Yemenite Jew walked the streets barefoot wearing plaid cotton pants and a ten-gallon hat from Texas.

(Ari Ibn-Zahav, Shishim Shanah veShanah)

Fewer and fewer people remained in Jerusalem. Many died of hunger and disease, and many left the city for the coastal areas or left the country altogether. Before the war, there were 45,000 Jews in Jerusalem; after the war, there remained but 34,000.

Wash day in old Jerusalem

1917   1948

1000

The British Take Control

At the end of 1917, when the British Army, under the command of General Allenby, arrived in Jerusalem, the entire Turkish garrison fled the city in one night. The next day, two British sergeants left their camp at the village of Lifta near Jerusalem to try and find fresh eggs for their commanding officer's breakfast. On their way, they bumped into a group of Arab dignitaries. As it happened, these were the mayor of Jerusalem and his entourage on their way to surrender Jerusalem to the commander of the victorious army. The sergeants forgot about the eggs and brought the mayor to their commander, who accepted the surrender.

Two days later, on the eleventh of December 1917, General Allenby entered the Old City of Jerusalem at the head of his troops and representatives of various other countries. When the General reached the Jaffa Gate, he dismounted his horse and entered the holy city on foot, to symbolize his recognition of the religious and historic significance of Jerusalem. Thus ended four hundred years of Turkish rule in Jerusalem.

The League of Nations, predecessor of the United Nations, granted the government of Britain a mandate (responsibility) to administer the affairs of the land of Israel. From then on, Jerusalem became the capital of the British Mandatory Government in the land of Israel. The British called the country Palestine, adopting the name first used by the Romans nearly 2,000 years previously.

General Allenby

General Allenby, entering Jerusalem triumphantly (1917)

-1000

0

Mahaneh Yehudah Market

Words cannot describe the joy of Jerusalem's inhabitants when the British Army entered the city. The people emerged from their hiding places. . . to walk the streets without fear. A few days earlier, no one would have dared to leave his house to walk in the street, for fear the Turkish police would demand identification papers and send anyone who had deserted or not served in the army straight to the local military commander. . . . Today, though, everyone walked about freely, in small groups. We began walking up Jaffa Road. . ., and we saw how quiet it was and realized what a great miracle the Holy One had performed for us, the residents of the holy city of Jerusalem. . . .

On our way back, when we arrived at the Mahaneh Yehudah neighborhood, we saw that the grocery stores had already opened, that we could already purchase groceries, and that the Jews were preparing for Hanukah. That night we lit the first Hanukah candle and recited the Shehehiyanu: "Blessed are You, O Eternal our God, who has sustained us and kept us alive and brought us to this moment."

(Rafael Hayyim haKohen, Avanim baHomah)

The Jews rejoiced at the British conquest of the city for an additional reason. During the war, as the result of contacts between the Zionist Movement and the British government, the British had issued a document known as the Balfour Declaration. The document was signed by Lord Arthur Balfour, the British Foreign Secretary; in it, His Majesty's Government promised the Jews a national home in Palestine.

His Majesty's Government view with favour the establishment in Palestine of a national home for the Jewish people, and will use their best endeavours to facilitate the achievement of this object, it being clearly understood that nothing shall be done which may prejudice the civil and religious rights of existing non-Jewish communities in Palestine, or the rights and political status enjoyed by Jews in any other country.

105

1000   1917   1948

Lord Herbert Samuel

After the British entered the city, the Jews held an impressive ceremony for General Allenby and his men in a hall in the Bukharan Quarter, that had been built to receive the Messiah.

In 1920, the British government appointed Herbert Samuel, an English Jew, as the High Commissioner for Palestine.

In the Hebrew month of Tamuz, we heard that a Jew named Herbert Samuel was appointed High Commissioner for Palestine. The joy of the Jews throughout the country was so great that it cannot be described. In the month of Av, the British battleship arrived at the port of Jaffa. The High Commissioner arrived on the shore dressed in his official uniform, and the Jews saw him as the true Redeemer. Happiness and joy reigned throughout the land, the ship fired a twenty-one gun salute in his honor. He was received here with the honor befitting a king, and afterward, he boarded a train to Jerusalem. The people of the city came out to greet him, and when he passed in his car, the entire crowd roared in joy, and he was received with great cheering.

On Sabbath Nahamu [the Sabbath following the fast of the Ninth of Av], he was invited to pray at the Hurvat Rabbi Yehudah heHasid Synagogue. To this service were invited the Ashkenazi and Sephardi chief rabbis and heads of the rabbinic courts and every important person and dignitary of every Jewish community in Jerusalem. . . . I, too, was invited [as representative of the Persian Jewish community]. . . . He entered the synagogue to great cheering. . . . Herbert Samuel was honored with maftir [the final aliyah and reading from the prophets], and when he went up to the Torah, the entire congregation stood in his honor. After the Torah reading, he chanted the prophetic portion, Nahamu nahamu: Be comforted, be comforted, My people (Isaiah 40:1ff). . . .

(Rafael Hayyim haKohen, Avanim baHomah)

Lord Samuel at the Hurvah Synagogue

-1000

0

The National Struggle for Jerusalem

The Jews' euphoria was premature. As it turned out, the British government had made promises concerning the land of Israel not only to the Jews but to the Arabs as well. The Arabs saw the land of Israel as belonging to them and Jerusalem as a city holy to Islam, third in importance to Mecca and Medina. They tried in different ways to oppose the development of a Jewish community in the country, particularly in Jerusalem. They held demonstrations, attacked individual Jews and Jewish neighborhoods, burned stores and motor vehicles, and tried in every possible way to disrupt Jewish life in the city.

A fierce struggle developed over the Western Wall. The Jews prayed there, and the Arabs harassed them. They demanded, for instance, that Jews be forbidden to sound the shofar at the Western Wall, and the British authorities acceded to their demand.

In 1931, Rabbi Moshe Segal was a security guard in the vineyards of the village of Rehovot. When he heard of the British decree against sounding the shofar at the Western Wall at the end of Yom Kippur, he decided that this could not be: he would go to Jerusalem and sound his shofar at the wall. And if they arrested him? Let them arrest him!

Rabbi Abraham Yitzhak Hacohen Kook

Segal concealed his shofar under his tallit, and when the first stars appeared signifying the end of the fast, he took out his shofar and gave a great blast. British police arrived on the scene immediately and arrested him.

Moshe Segal had studied with the legendary Avraham Yitzhak Kook, Chief Rabbi of the land of Israel. When Rav Kook heard that his student had been detained by the police, he announced that he would not eat but rather continue the fast of Yom Kippur until Segal's release. The British, who wished to avoid controversy, responded by freeing Segal. In later years too, there was always someone to sound the shofar at the Western Wall.

(Menahem Barash-Ro'i, Besodam Shel Yakirei Yerushalayim)

Rabbi Moshe Segal (with talit) holding the Shofar

1917   1948

1000

Shemuel Yosef Agnon
"books pulled down,
scattered and torn"

*Over the years of the British Mandate, there were
quiet periods, but there were also periods of harsh
confrontation - Arab riots, as they came to be called -
which resulted in Jewish injuries and deaths:*

*Again, shooting at night. Not a single night passes
without it. People lie like empty sacks, blood-covered in
a bullet-ridden car in the street, in their work rooms in
outlying neighbourhoods. A young couple on the street.
A family in a private house on the slope that goes down
to the city. More shooting. Who will it be now?
Where? People stay locked in their houses, silent,
listening to the night. Police. An ambulance. Silence.*

*The city is wounded, gasping, grieving. . . evil stalks
the streets. Children pull blankets over their heads,
afraid to close their eyes, until conquered by an
anguished sleep that offers no rest.
Young Arabs hold demonstrations in the streets and sing
their battle songs calling for jihad - holy war - against
the Jews: "We will go to jihad eagerly, we will go to
jihad in a storm, we will go to jihad with the flag of
revenge!"*

(Shulamit Hareven, Ir Yamim Rabbim)

*Arabs attacked Jewish neighborhoods, plundering and
destroying homes, killing and injuring residents. One
of the houses attacked belonged to the noted author
Shemuel Yosef Agnon (who in 1966 was awarded the
Nobel Prize for literature):*

*The entire household was turned upside down, and
the sense of destruction this produced is indescribable.
Three thousand books. . . pulled down, scattered and
torn; and from among them peeks an ancient
Hagaddah, handwritten, with large letters calling,
"And we cried out to the God of our fathers, and He
saw our distress" - this is what the letters shouted from
that page.*

(Shemuel Yosef Agnon, meAtzmi El Atzmi)

-1000

0

The Jews Organize to Defend Themselves and Attack

For various political reasons, the British government gave preference in many cases to the Arab interests, and did not always curb Arab violence. In 1920, after the Arabs attacked the Jews of the city and many Jews were wounded and killed, the Jews established a secret organization known as the Haganah - Hebrew for "defense" - whose aim it was to defend Jews when attacked. In many cases, the Haganah managed to frustrate attacks on Jews. The Haganah was supported by the majority of Jews living in Palestine; over the years, it developed into an underground army and ultimately the foundation for Zahal, the Israel Defense Forces.

Haganah members and the oath of loyalty

A young Jerusalemite tells how he and his friends joined the Haganah. It was after a regular meeting of his youth group in 1932:

After the discussion, the leaders said we had to go to a "rendez-vous somewhere."
They brought me to the Community Council building at the corner of haNevi'im and Rav Kook Streets. They made us all sit in the entry hall. We were twenty, twenty-five teenagers. There, at the Community Council, they told us in whispers that we were being inducted to the Haganah.

I find it difficult to describe the excitement and trepidation that gripped me. Membership in the Haganah seemed exalted, beyond my capability; I wasn't certain I was worthy. An aura of holiness enveloped the whole organization, and with it, the knowledge that, here in this place, a person pledges his

life - that from now on, his life belongs not to him alone, but that he himself, together with everything he owns, his meager possessions, is ready to answer any call.

I entered. A darkened room opened before me. The only light came from a dim oil lamp on the table. . . . Around the table sat people bundled in coats, dark: secretive characters, whom I could not identify.

"Why have you come? What do you want here?

"I came to join the Haganah."

(Moshe Adaki, beEsh Netzurah)

1917 1948

1000

Generali building built during the
British Mandate Period

In addition to the Haganah, there were two other
underground organizations, both of which favored
active military struggle against the British. These
were the Irgun Tzva'i Le'umi (National Military
Organization), abbreviated as "Etzel" and often
known simply as "the Irgun"; and Lohamei Herut
Yisrael (Israel Freedom Fighters), abbreviated
as "Lehi." These two
organizations attacked the
British army with the
objective of forcing the British
government to leave the land
of Israel so that a Jewish state
could arise. In 1946,
members of the Etzel blew up
the headquarters of the British
army in the King David Hotel
in Jerusalem. This act was a
violation of the Haganah's
policy, which opposed terror
and concentrated on
defending the Jewish
population.

King David Hotel
after the
explosion

-1000

0

The Development of Jerusalem and the Jewish Population of Palestine under the British Mandate

The British authorities greatly improved the city of Jerusalem by introducing modern municipal facilities and procedures long prevalent in the cities of Europe. They prepared master plans to facilitate construction of neighborhoods and public buildings in an orderly fashion; they built a city water system and introduced electricity; and they saw to the disposal of waste and sewage. During the Mandate, administrative and cultural buildings (such as the High Commissioner's residence - Armon haNetziv - and the Rockefeller Museum of archaeology) were constructed; as were hotels (such as the King David); many schools; and Jewish and Arab neighborhoods.

As is well known, all structures in Jerusalem must be built of stone. What is the source of this law? The British saw that the Jewish population of Jerusalem was growing rapidly, because many of those who immigrated to the country chose to settle in Jerusalem. The British wished to restrain the expansion of Jerusalem's Jewish population without saying so directly. Thus, they issued a building ordinance prohibiting construction of walls in Jerusalem of mud, tin, and other materials. Since concrete was not yet available, the only remaining material was stone. Stone, however, is expensive and requires more construction time; it was thought that this additional expense would deter people from building their homes in Jerusalem. Moreover, most of those involved in quarrying and dressing the Jerusalem limestone were Arabs, and this made the Jews dependent on the Arabs.

(Meir Ben Dov, Atlas Carta Yerushalayim biRe'i haDorot)

Despite this limitation, Jerusalem's Jewish population grew steadily. During the British Mandate (1917-1948), the number of Jews in Jerusalem grew from 34,000 to 99,000, and Jews constituted 60% of the city's population. The construction in stone, the purpose of which was to restrain the city's growth, has given Jerusalem her famous golden glow at sunrise and sunset, a beauty which distinguishes it from all other cities in Israel.

Typical Jerusalem architecture: arches and Jerusalem limestone

1917   1948

1000

Jerusalem and Plans to Partition Palestine

In 1927, the Binyan haMosedot haLe'umiyim, the National Institutions Building, was erected to house the central offices of the Zionist leadership of the "Yishuv," the Jewish population of Palestine. Together, the offices in this building formed a kind of pre-state Israeli government. Other important institutions, such as the Hebrew University on Mount Scopus, the Jewish National and University Library, and the Chief Rabbinate, were also established in Jerusalem, emphasizing the city's centrality to the Jewish people and the Zionist Movement.

The inability of the British authorities to put an end to the tensions and hostilities between the Jews and Arabs led to the idea of dividing the country between the two peoples. Various divisions were suggested based upon settlement patterns - the Arabs to receive areas of dense Arab settlement and the Jews to receive the areas they had settled. In each of these plans, the most problematic issue was Jerusalem. The British suggested on various occasions that Jerusalem remain under their control, and that they would protect the rights of all religious groups in the city. The Arabs opposed every type of partition plan; they claimed that the entire country belonged to them, and that no part of it should be awarded to the Jews. The Jewish leadership, however, accepted the idea of partition, because they felt that it was better to receive a small country that could absorb Jews suffering from persecution all over the world, than to demand everything at once - which they thought they had no chance of receiving.

The National Institutions Building, home of the Jewish Agency

The question of Palestine was finally handed over to the United Nations, and on the twenty-ninth of November, 1947, the UN decided that the British must leave the country and that Palestine would be divided between Jews and Arabs. The majority of Palestine west of the Jordan would be given to the Jews and a smaller part to the Arabs. Jerusalem was to receive the special status of an International City administered by the UN. The reason for this was Jerusalem's holiness to the three monotheistic religions: Judaism, Christianity, and Islam. The UN did not wish to give control of Jerusalem to any one religious group.

The leaders of the Jewish community - David Ben Gurion and the others - agreed to this arrangement, feeling they had no choice, but the Arabs rejected it. Spurning all plans to partition the country and internationalize Jerusalem, they declared war against the Jews of Palestine.

THE WAR OF INDEPENDENCE -
JERUSALEM DIVIDED

The End of the British Mandate: The Struggle for Jerusalem Begins

On the twenty-ninth of November 1947, the United Nations voted to partition Palestine into separate Jewish and Arab states. Immediately afterward, local Arab bands began attacking the Jews all over the country. Several days after the UN's decision, an Arab mob burst through the Jaffa Gate of the Old City, fell upon the Jewish commercial center on Mamilla Street, looted the stores, and burned them down. In many places, Arab snipers shot at passers-by and into homes. Bombs were thrown, and cars loaded with explosives were detonated in Jewish neighborhoods; stores on Ben Yehudah Street (the present day downtown pedestrian mall) and the National Institutions Building were blown up.

The various Jewish defense organizations tried to protect the population and mounted counter attacks against Arab-held buildings. Although the British were still in Jerusalem, chaos reigned as the two sides prepared for all-out war. The British army gradually reduced its presence in the city and regrouped in a number of buildings and streets in the center of town, near the main post office.

The battle to open the road to Jerusalem

The Ben Yehudah Street explosion (Feb. 12, 1948)

-1000   0

The Siege of Jerusalem

An eyewitness recalls:

On the fourteenth of May, one day before the end of the Mandate, . . . at six in the morning, I saw a small car driven by a British sergeant pass among several buildings and stop at their entrances. At each stop, the sergeant would signal the sentries to get into the car. When they were all inside, six or eight soldiers all told, the car turned towards the post office, and from there to the eastern portion of the city. Thus, quietly and without ceremony, did the British administration, after thirty years, come to an end.

The Haganah had anticipated this moment, and immediately after the car disappeared, men rushed forward and seized all the buildings. By the time the Arabs arrived, the Haganah had already managed to fortify itself in its new positions and was able to repel them. That is how Arab access to Jaffa Road and the surrounding Jewish neighborhoods was prevented.

(Pinhas Pick, Idan II)

As soon as the British left, the regular armies of the Arab states bordering on Israel invaded the country. In Jerusalem, the Jewish forces found themselves mainly up against the Arab Legion (the army of Trans-Jordan) and, to a lesser extent, the Egyptian army. At that time, the Israel Defense Forces, Israel's regular army (Zahal in Hebrew), was just getting organized.

The Jews of Jerusalem received foodstuffs, such as flour, meat, fruit and vegetables, from the Jewish agricultural settlements in the coastal areas and the North. These supplies were transported by truck and rail, while water was piped in from the foothills. With the intensification of Arab hostilities, it became nearly impossible to transport the supplies essential for the maintenance of Jerusalem's population. For almost its entire length, the road from Tel Aviv to Jerusalem was flanked by Arab villages, whose residents would attack the Jewish transports trying to reach the capital. The pumping stations that pumped water to Jerusalem were also in Arab hands. Thus, Jerusalem found herself without food or water. The little food in the city was divided among families according to their size, and rations were extremely meager. Every person received coupons for the amount he was entitled to purchase, such as 150 grams (about 5 ounces) of bread per day, or seven eggs, half a kilo (1.1 pounds) of frozen meat, 400 grams (about 14 ounces) of margarine per week and so forth. Kerosene, used to fuel primitive cooking burners, was so scarce it was distributed in cups. The city administration proposed to its besieged population a method for conserving water.

A Glass of Water

I had a glass of water, one whole glass
When Jerusalem was under siege.

I swallowed a few drops, one or two,
Enough to moisten my lips.
I had a glass of water
In besieged Jerusalem.

With what was left I brushed my teeth
I even laundered my trousers every second month.
After my trousers, some water remained
Enough to wash my socks.

And then to wash my feet.
After two months I washed the floor.
With the water I squeezed from the mop,
I watered one potted rose, and one more.

(Dan Almagor)

In the open fields among the city's neighborhoods grew a wild plant named helmit, parts of which are edible. For this reason, the plant is known among the Arabs as hubz or hubeza-bread. For lack of other food, the children of Jerusalem would go out and gather the leaves and fruits of the hubz and bring them home. Mothers invented recipes for hubeza salad and hubeza patties.

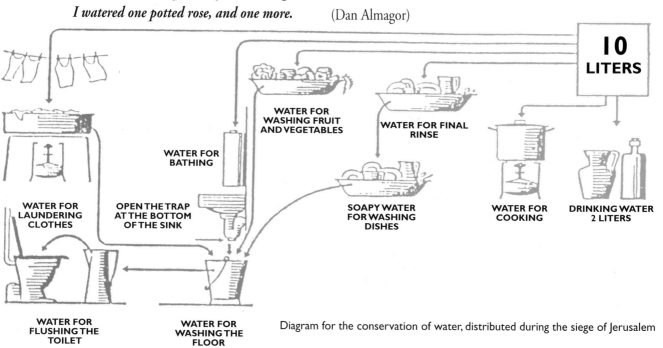

Diagram for the conservation of water, distributed during the siege of Jerusalem

Battles in Jerusalem

At the edge of Jewish Jerusalem, near the High Commissioner's residence (Armon haNetziv), there was a farm where young people received training before being sent to agricultural settlements. Rahel Yana'it Ben Zvi, the director, tells of life on the farm, where eighty young men and women studied during this difficult period.

In the winter of 1948, the pipe that supplied us (and the High Commissioner's residence) with water was blown up. We had to endanger the children and permit them to go down by night to draw water from the water tower, . . . using buckets tied to ropes. Our children were nimble and, dressed in black, they tiptoed up the ladder and passed up the buckets.

(Rahel Yana'it Ben Zvi, Idan II)

Throughout this time, fierce battles raged in Jerusalem - with each side trying to fortify its positions and capture parts of the city controlled by the other side. The Arab Legion (the army of Trans-Jordan) took up positions on the hills surrounding Jerusalem and shelled the Jewish sections. Thousands of shells fell on Jerusalem, destroying buildings, wounding a thousand residents and killing 200.

Exploiting every drop of water

1000

1948 1967

Since last night, the enemy has been raining artillery fire without interruption upon the Beit Yisrael and Meah She'arim neighborhoods. . . . The bombardment was particularly heavy against the northern neighborhoods (such as Sanhedria) and the western neighborhoods, but the center of town also suffered greatly. For the last two weeks, life in Jerusalem, with thousands of shells and hundreds of casualties, has been [life] in the midst of death.

The shelling of Jerusalem's neighborhoods was even heavier today than yesterday, which was a very difficult day. It seems as though the hours of the day are measured by the explosions of shells, which tick off the minutes like a clock of death. . . .

(Yeshurun Keshet, Idan II)

Jewish Quarter residents are rounded up for evacuation

During the battles in Jerusalem, the Jews managed to take control of most of the city, to defend the Jewish neighborhoods, and capture a number of Arab neighborhoods, but their success was not complete: there were battles in which the Arabs won.
The greatest failure was in the Jewish Quarter of the Old City. Some 1,300 Jews lived there, most of them old and impoverished. The Jewish leadership sent fighters to defend them, but they were insufficient in number to repel the Arab attackers. After a six-month siege, when all food and ammunition had run out, and after there remained only a handful of fighters who had not been wounded, the Jews were forced to surrender. The Arabs sent the old people, women and children to the Jewish sector of the city, but took 290 young men to a prison camp in Trans-Jordan. There they remained until the end of the war.

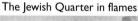

The Jewish Quarter in flames

The Convoys to Jerusalem

The Jews of Jerusalem sometimes felt that their brothers in the other parts of the country, particularly the government sitting in Tel Aviv, had simply forgotten about them. But, despite the great difficulties involved in coming to her aid, the Jews of Israel never forgot Jerusalem. On numerous occasions, Jewish leaders expressed the eternal connection between the Jewish people and Jerusalem.

If this land has a soul, Jerusalem is its soul. . . . Jerusalem demands, and deserves, that we stand with her. The oath that our fathers swore by the rivers of Babylon [If I forget thee, O Jerusalem, may my right hand lose its cunning], binds us today as it did then. If we fail Jerusalem, we will not be worthy of the name Israel.

(David Ben Gurion, Prime Minister of Israel)

I hereby declare that the entire Knesset is united in its resolution that Jerusalem is an inseparable part of the State of Israel. In no way may any foreign government be imposed on her.

(Yosef Sprinzak, Speaker of the Knesset)

The Jews of Israel did not confine themselves to fine words, they did all they could to alleviate the suffering of the residents of Jerusalem and guarantee that the city would indeed be part of the Jewish state. When the Arabs cut off its passage to the coast, convoys were sent to transport supplies in large quantities, and these convoys were escorted by fighters and armored vehicles in order to ensure that they reach their destination.

Getting through to Jerusalem, however, was by no means simple. The Arabs fired on the convoys from their strategically located villages and positions on the mountain tops, disabling vehicles and wounding the people inside them. Trucks went up in flames and many of the drivers and members of the escort were killed. Sometimes, part of the supplies and ammunition reached the city, but on many occasions the convoys were forced to return to their base without getting through. Particularly fierce attacks were mounted at Sha'ar haGai (in Arabic, Bab el-Wad), the narrow mountain pass leading up through the Judean Hills to Jerusalem.

119

1948 1967

1000

The rain of bullets that struck our convoy at the entrance to Sha'ar haGai surprised everyone. No one expected such a warm reception. . . . trucks were hit one after the other. They [the Arabs] had learned the trick. . . . first you shoot out the tires, and then the target can no longer move. From then on, you snipe at it at your leisure. . . . the sixth truck of the convoy was hit. The driver seemed to have lost control. It was listing to its side and about to turn over, and it blocked the way of the rest of the convoy. . . . black smoke began rising from the cabin, and cries for help could be heard.

(Aharon Almog, Shavu'a beTashah)

Jerusalem remained under siege all during the winter and spring. One of the most dangerous points for the convoys trying to break through was where the road passed under the Jordanian positions at the Latrun Monastery. In June of 1948, Israeli soldiers accidently discovered a new way through the mountains. The steep and winding path was outside the range of the Jordanian guns and might be passable for motor vehicles . At first, supplies were carried over this route on the backs of soldiers and pack animals. At the same time, the Israeli forces worked feverishly to improve it until finally it could be used by the convoys. A new water pipe to Jewish Jerusalem was also laid along this road.

Remembering the alternate road to China cut through Burma by the British in World War II, Israeli soldiers dubbed this new route the "Burma Road." The Burma Road was the first important step in relieving Jerusalem's plight.

Conquering the Villages That Attacked the Convoys

When the commanders of the Haganah saw that it was impossible to move supplies to Jerusalem, even in armed convoys, they decided to change tactics: they attacked and captured the villages that controlled the road from the mountain tops. From then on, it was possible to travel safely: the siege of Jerusalem was broken.

This burnt-out vehicle opened the road to beleaguered Jerusalem in 1948, left as a memorial by the roadside

Chaim Guri's poem "Bab el-Wad" commemorates the men and women who rode the convoys and fought their way to Jerusalem - those who made it through and those who did not. The poem was subsequently set to music and became one of the classics of Israel's War of Independence.

Suddenly, at dawn on Friday, we were told to assemble at the bus stop in Tel Aviv, because in another half hour, we would move. . . . the convoy was very, very long, and dozens of vehicles loaded with food and equipment moved out slowly. All day and all night we traveled. The wheels groaned; the people were quiet. Along the roadside, we saw the burnt-out armored trucks, and wondered if our fate would be the same. And then we arrived at the Judean Mountains, and on the roof of the water pumping station on the way to Jerusalem a flag was flying - blue and white! A wave of joy and pride washed our hearts. Our flag! For the first time, we breathed easily. And indeed, at eight in the morning, on Shabbat itself, we arrived at the gates of Jerusalem.

(Shoshanah Har'eli, Yalkut Yerushalayim)

Bab el-Wad!

Let our names be remembered forever.

Convoys cutting through to the city.

By the roadside lie our fallen.

A *burnt-out truck lies quiet, like my friend.*

Bab el-Wad,

Let our names be remembered forever,

Bab el-Wad

On the way to Jerusalem.

(Chaim Guri)

Jerusalem Divided Between Israel and Jordan

On the thirtieth of November, 1948, one year after the struggle for Jerusalem began, a cease-fire agreement was signed between Jordan and Israel in Jerusalem. The negotiators drew lines on a map according to the placement of Israeli and Jordanian fortifications. The lines ran north and south and divided Jerusalem into eastern and western sectors with a narrow strip of "no man's land" in between. The Jews held the western sector of the city plus the Hadassah Hospital and the Hebrew University on Mount Scopus (overlooking Jerusalem from the east), while the Jordanians held the Old City and various other Arab neighborhoods adjoining it on the north, east and south. From the time the agreement was signed until the reunification of Jerusalem in 1967, there was no free passage between the Jordanian and Israeli sectors.

Since Mount Scopus and its structures remained in Jewish hands, while the road to Mount Scopus was held by Jordan, the accords provided that every two weeks a convoy would travel to the Jewish enclave on Mount Scopus to replace the soldiers who guarded it. The Old City and the Western Wall, of course, remained in Jordanian hands, and the agreement established that Jews would be permitted to pray at the Western Wall. This, however, did not come to pass. For the nineteen years of Jordanian rule over the Old City, Jews were not permitted access to the Western Wall.

Now a border passed through the heart of Jerusalem, and Israeli and Jordanian soldiers faced each other from opposite sides. Barbed wire fences prevented passage from one side of the city to the other. From time to time, Jordanian soldiers fired on Israeli soldiers and citizens. In order to prevent casualties, concrete walls were built at the most dangerous spots to protect the residents, and signs that read "Danger! Border Ahead!" were placed all along the line.

Jerusalem divided

-1000

0

On the Roof of Notre Dame

The roof of Notre Dame was my own Mount Nebo
I could see the Holy sites but not come near.
Those little rectangles on the Mount of Olives
Mark the graves of my fallen brothers
Whom no one has visited for five years
With prayer or wreath.

And they're all so close. . .
Reach out your hand and grasp them:
Jaffa Gate. . . Damascus Gate
But so far, like a passing dream.
Come down from the roof and it all disappears. . .
All, but a slight tingling at the base of your fingers
All, but the gritting of teeth and the build-up of tears.

(Yitzhak Shalev*)*

Along the border stretched rusty barbed wire; all sorts of discarded objects and junk accumulated between its coils. Moss pushed its way through the hillocks of earth that had been piled up, and on the other side of the barbed wire stretched a strip known as "no man's land" dotted with abandoned houses in various states of disrepair and deterioration.

(David Shahar, Moto Shel Elohim haKatan)

Mount of Olives

Jerusalemites and tourists who wanted to see something of the Old City would climb onto the roofs of tall buildings and gaze into eastern Jerusalem.

Differences in the Development of the City's Two Sectors

The government of Jordan invested little in Jerusalem during the years that it controlled the city's eastern half. The reason was clear: the center of the Jordanian state was in Amman, on the East Bank of the Jordan, and so it was clearly in that country's interest to award priority to its own capital.

One project was undertaken in those days, and the impression it left on the city remains to this day. It was under Jordanian rule that the two domes on the Temple Mount - the Dome of the Rock and the Al Aksa Mosque - were covered in gold and silver respectively.

This was in sharp contrast to the situation in west Jerusalem. The government did much for the city, as befits its status as capital of the country. Thousands of new immigrants settled in the city, first in ma'abarot, primitive transit camps built to handle the flood of new arrivals, and later in permanent housing hurriedly built for them. In 1966, Jewish Jerusalem had 190,000 residents, as opposed to 60,000 residents in the Jordanian sector.

During the years that Jerusalem was divided, government, cultural, and educational institutions - such as the Hebrew University's Givat Ram campus, the Jewish National and University Library, the Hadassah Hospital, Heikhal Shlomo (seat of the Chief Rabbinate) and the Israel Museum - were built in west Jerusalem. Various symbolic activities also highlighted Jerusalem as the capital of the Zionist state and the Jewish homeland. These included transfer of the remains of Theodore Herzl from Vienna to Mount Herzl, and the establishment of Yad Vashem, the Holocaust Memorial Authority, nearby.

124

A transit camp (ma'abara) in Jerusalem

THE SIX DAY WAR - JERUSALEM REUNITED

THE SIX DAY WAR-JERUSALEM REUNITED

The Six Day War

The Arab nations refused to accept Israel's existence. From time to time fighting would break out, with clashes ranging from border incidents to all-out war. In 1956, Israel fought the Sinai Campaign against Egypt, and again in 1967, tension between Israel and her neighbors exploded into war on the fifth of June.

Hostilities began in Jerusalem, when the Jordanian army opened fire all along the section of its border with Israel that passed through the heart of the city. Shooting started at 10:45 am, and Israel launched its counter-attack shortly thereafter. Units of the Israel Defense Forces fought difficult, hand-to-hand battles at Ammunition Hill, linked up to Mount Scopus, and broke through to the Old City. In two days of fierce fighting, the Israeli army captured all of Jordan's positions in Jerusalem and the surrounding area. One hundred eighty-three soldiers fell in the battles for Jerusalem, and many more were wounded.

The Israel Defense Forces captured the Old City on the 28th of the Hebrew month of Iyar, 5727 (7 June 1967). The date was subsequently proclaimed Jerusalem Day, on which the Jewish people celebrates the city's unification.

Map labels: Atarot Airport, Neveh Ya'akov, Pisgat Ze'ev, Ramot, Mt. Scopus, Me'ah She'arim, Hadassah Hospital, Rehaviah, Old City, Kiryat Yovel, Gilo, Talpiot

Municipal Jerusalem Today

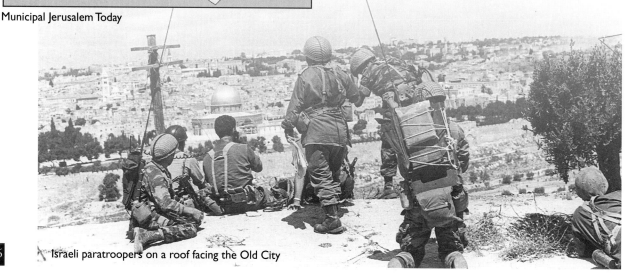

Israeli paratroopers on a roof facing the Old City

-1000   0

. . . Even the ordinary soldier
Whose blood fell upon the ancient path
Knew
That the splendor of Mountains,
the silvery treetops,
And the glittering dome
Are the outer gold
Of the song of Solomon and of David's tear.

(Zelda)

At the Western Wall

The command came to move. The commander's half-track zoomed towards the Lions' Gate. Right behind, the rest of the troops sped ahead through the blackened arch of the Lions' Gate. . . .

We arrive at the Mosque of Omar (the golden Dome of the Rock). From here to the Western Wall, it's only an extremely short distance. Men press forward quickly over the paving stones, as though pushed by a storm wind. Hearts pound; the excitement is tremendous. We are among the first to arrive at a small gate. From here, narrow, winding stairs lead us to the Western Wall. The Western Wall! Last remnant of the Temple. No Jew has set foot here for nineteen years. We are pushed ahead by the rising tide of soldiers. . . hundreds of dusty, perspiring paratroopers, their clothing stained with blood, crowd into the narrow rectangle in front of the Wall. . . . Hardened men, who for two solid days have waged war in pitched and bloody battles heavy with casualties, crying out loud with no shame - crying in excitement and release, in exaltation and recognition of the greatness and eternity of the Jewish people.

(Yosef Argaman, Bamahaneh, magazine of the Israel Defense Forces)

1000

1967   1996

Excerpt from a Radio Broadcast Heard throughout Israel:

- Reporter, Rafa'el Amir was with the troops that broke through to the Old City this morning (in the background - sounds of heavy vehicles and shooting).

- (Soldier's voice filled with emotion heard over military shortwave radio) "The Temple Mount (shooting in the background) is ours! This is Talmi [the shortwave radio operator's last name], the Temple Mount is ours, over. The Temple Mount is ours (shouts of soldiers; in the background, heavy vehicles and soldiers shouting). . . .

- We are in the Old City. We are in the Old City. The soldiers flatten themselves against the walls. We are moving along the Via Dolorosa (in the background, sounds of a shofar, heavy vehicles, and soldiers shouting). Do you understand?! The Old City! (the reporter's voice is choked with tears). We are in the Old City!

- (Voices of soldiers) The Wall. Lets go up to the Wall.

- To the Wall.

- (Loud cheering of soldiers.)

- (Sounds of the shofar and soldiers singing Yerushalayim shel Zahav.)

- (Reporter in voice choked with tears): At this moment, I am descending the stairs that lead to the Wall. A moment more, and I will be at the Wall (weeps out loud).

- (The sounds of soldiers shouting and Rabbi Goren, Chief Army Chaplain, praying.)

- (Rabbi Goren recites the benediction, and the soldiers respond): Barukh Atah haShem, Elokeinu, Melekh ha'olam, shehehiyannu, vekiyemannu, vehigiyannu lazeman hazeh (Blessed are You, O Eternal our God, Who has kept us alive, sustained us, and brought us to this time)!

- Amen!

(Recorded by the Israel Broadcast Authority)

The late Rabbi Goren, Chief Rabbi of the Israel Defense Forces, sounds the shofar as the Western Wall is liberated

A few months before the outbreak of the Six Day War, Naomi Shemer's song "Yerushalayim Shel Zahav" ["Jerusalem of Gold"] was played for the first time in Israel. This is the song the soldiers sang spontaneously in the emotion-filled first moments after they reached the Western Wall. The chorus is well known:

Jerusalem of gold, of copper and of light.
Behold I am a harp for all your songs.

When "Jerusalem of Gold," was first composed, however, Jews were still unable to reach the Old City. Thus she lamented:

How dry are your cisterns
How empty your market and square.
No one visits the Temple Mount
In the Old City.

In the caves of your rocks
How the wind does howl.
And no one can reach the Dead Sea
By way of Jericho.

Neither Naomi Shemer nor anyone else dreamed that, only a few months after the song was broadcast, Jews would be able to stroll through the Old City and drive directly to the Dead Sea via Jericho. After the Six Day War, therefore, she added the following verse:

We have returned to the cisterns,
To the market and the square;
The shofar calls on the Temple Mount
In the Old City.
And from the caves in the rocks
A thousand suns shine forth.
Again we will go down to the Dead Sea
By way of Jericho

(Naomi Shemer)

Soldiers fighting on the southern front, in Sinai and Gaza heard of Jerusalem's capture over the radio. One of them recalls:

Afterward, they played "Jerusalem of Gold." We were so filled with emotion, that the entire battalion joined in. I was overjoyed; everyone was overjoyed. We forgot for that moment of the loss of life it had cost us. . . . This, in my opinion, was the high point of the war. For us, this was the greatest moment of the Six Day War.

(Moshe Natan, haMilhamah Al Yerushalayim)

The Temple, an imaginary drawing by Chaim Ron

That same day, Levi Eshkol, Prime Minister of Israel, arrived at the Western Wall and declared:

"It is a great historical privilege to be standing here at this time at the Western Wall, last remnant of our holy Temple and our historic past. I see myself as representative of the entire people, as the representative of many generations of our people who longed for Jerusalem and her holiness. . . . From Jerusalem, eternal capital of Israel, I send a blessing of peace and security to all the citizens of Israel and to all our Jewish brothers wherever they may be. Blessed is He who has kept us alive, sustained us, and brought us to this time."

Twenty years have passed since last I visited the Western Wall with my father. Now I come with my five-year old daughter on my shoulder.

Why have I brought her here? Why did my father, who was not even religious, bother to bring me to the Western Wall when I was a child? Why have hundreds of thousands of Jews come to the Western Wall since the Old City was liberated?

Because we missed it. That's the reason. We missed the Western Wall, and we loved it. It is the only complete remnant that has remained of the Temple, it saw the Temple in all its glory, and it was a witness to its destruction, our destruction. . . . The Western Wall is not merely a symbol of the past, it also symbolizes the future, and the hope. For the day will come when all Jews will gather here, the Temple will be rebuilt, and the Kingdom of David will be restored.

(Shemuel, haAretz Shelanu)

A colorful view of the Western Wall by Salvador Dali

-1000   0

Reunification and Development

Immediately after the capture of the eastern sector of Jerusalem, measures were taken to reunite the two halves of the city. Military positions were dismantled. Ruined buildings that stood in the no-man's land left over from the 1948 War of Independence were demolished. Fences and walls dividing the city were removed, roads abruptly truncated during the War of Independence, were rejoined. The city's boundaries were greatly expanded, and this contributed to its development. Jerusalem ceased to be a border town, and security improved greatly. Many Jews immigrated to Israel in the years following the Six Day War; many made their homes in Jerusalem.

A new era has begun in the history of the Jewish people. The Diaspora and Israel have discovered each other. Since the days of the Bar Kokhba Revolt, there has never been such complete unity between Israel and the Diaspora as there was now, during the Six Day War. In this, the Diaspora has chosen its course. The Diaspora must now transcend itself in spiritual nobility, and come to the land of Israel. . . . The land is wide open to the joy of creation, to the creation of a new world.

(Chaim Hazaz)

1000

The bus-route to Mt. Scopus reopens (1968)

There was tremendous growth in construction. Houses, whole neighborhoods, and communal buildings, such as the Jerusalem Theatre and the new-old Hebrew University campus on Mount Scopus, sprang up. Large parks were laid out. Hotels were built to accomodate the many tourists, whose numbers increased greatly after the city's unification. Many important archaeological excavations were undertaken, particularly in the vicinity of the Western Wall and other parts of the Old City. Ancient sites that were uncovered were restored and opened for visitation by thousands of tourists: the Herodian House, the Burnt House (remnants from the Second Temple period), the Cardo - an ancient Roman street and market place. A museum of the history of Jerusalem was established in David's Citadel near the Jaffa Gate.

Major projects were begun in the Old City. The narrow plaza in front of the Western Wall was greatly expanded to accomodate the vast number of Jews who came to visit there. The houses and synagogues of the Jewish Quarter of the Old City, destroyed during the War of Independence and the subsequent Jordanian occupation, were restored or rebuilt. The Jewish Quarter was again populated by Jews. Many synagogues, including the four old Sephardi synagogues and the Ramban (Nahmanides) synagogue were reconstructed and reopened for services.

Jerusalem's population grew, and the city became the largest city in Israel. In 1995, there were nearly 600,000 residents, 72% of whom were Jewish.

The Ben Zakkai Synagogue; in ruins in 1967 and after restoration

-1000

0

Contrast and Conflict

With the unification of the city and its expansion, divisions that had always existed among the main segments of Jerusalem's population were exacerbated. Jerusalem is home to an extremely diverse Jewish population: orthodox Jews of every conceivable shade, non-observant Jews with a broad range of outlooks, a wide variety of Jewish communities from East and West, and very large communities of new immigrants from all over the world, with American and Russian immigrants particularly prominent. The non-Jewish population is not less divided: Christian Arabs and Moslem Arabs, Armenians, and every imaginable Christian sect, ranging from Ethiopians and Catholics to Mormons. Such contrasts lead, not infrequently, to tensions, demonstrations, and even violence.

The problem of Jerusalem is a difficult one, because deep, long-standing emotions cloud the rational thought needed to resolve problems. Nevertheless, I am convinced that with the help of good will, these problems can be resolved.

Permit me to speak with complete candor: The thing I fear most is that this city, which is so beautiful, so filled with meaning, so holy to millions of people, will at some time in the future again be divided; that barbed wire, minefields, and concrete walls will again block its streets; that armed men will again patrol a border that passes through the city's heart. I fear a new division of the city not only as her mayor, as a Jew, and as an Israeli, but also as a man extremely sensitive to the city's history and one concerned with his entire being for the welfare of her inhabitants.

(Teddy Kollek, Mayor of Jerusalem)

Faces of Jerusalem

1967   1996

Basic Law: Jerusalem the Capital of Israel

1. Jerusalem, complete and united, is the capital of Israel.

2. Jerusalem is the seat of the President, the State, the Knesset, the Government, and the Supreme Court.

3. The Holy Places shall be protected from desecration and any other violation and from anything likely to violate the freedom of access of the members of the different religions to the places sacred to them or their feelings towards those places. . . .

The floral sun-dial near the Knesset

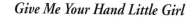

Give Me Your Hand Little Girl

Give me your hand, little girl
And we'll see Jerusalem.
Let us go by,
Through and around Jerusalem.

We'll look at the flowers
And walk on the wall,
Perhaps we'll meet kings
And who-knows-what-all.

Across from the Dung Gate
Under the shady pines
We'll stop a while
To see what goes on.

Perhaps we'll see God
In one place or two
For God is something you can see
Sometimes, in Jerusalem.

(Moshe Haneomi, Amarti leMiri)

JERUSALEM THE ETERNAL

Jerusalem the Eternal

"If I forget Thee, O Jerusalem" A multilayered papercut by Archie Granot, Jerusalem 1994

Since the days of David and Solomon, Jerusalem has become the most exalted symbol and expression of the oneness of the Jewish people and the land of Israel. The significance of Jerusalem to the Jewish people finds expression in the Bible -- in the words of the prophets and the songs of David -- and in the words of our Sages, authors, and poets in every generation. The future redemption of the Jewish people is symbolized in the redemption of Jerusalem. It is no coincidence that the redemptive movement of the Jewish people in modern times is called the Zionist Movement, named for Zion -- Jerusalem.

For almost two millennia, the Jewish people projected all its hopes and dreams, everything lost in expulsion and exile from its land, onto the Jerusalem of the future. Today some of these things are not mere fantasy but rather have become reality.

Jerusalem in the People's Consciousness

For many generations, the Jewish people remembered Jerusalem and hoped and prayed that she be speedily rebuilt.

Return in mercy to Your city Jerusalem and dwell in it as You have promised; rebuild it soon, in our days, as an everlasting edifice, and speedily establish in it the throne of David, Your servant.

(Amidah -- Sephardi and Ashkenazi rites)

Through the deserts of Diaspora you followed us, O Jerusalem. In every wilderness, we swore to follow you. On every gallows, you accompanied us, and our foremost blessing was always, "Next year in Jerusalem."

(David Shimoni)

Previous page: "Heavenly Jerusalem" (gouache), by Shemuel A. Katz

Generation after generation on Seder eve, on the holiday of our freedom, and in the Ne'ilah service of Yom Kippur -- on our greatest national holiday and our holiest religious holiday, Jews throughout the world have declared: "Next year in Jerusalem!" The word, "Jerusalem" embodies within it the entire land of Israel.

(Menahem Ussishkin)

The sense of connection with Jerusalem is expressed in emotions so intricately bound up with the Jewish soul that, though a Jew be born and live in the Diaspora, he can perceive himself as a native Jerusalemite. In 1966, Hebrew author, Shemuel Yosef Agnon, received the Nobel Prize for Literature. In his acceptance speech delivered in Stockholm, Sweden, he declared:
Let me tell you who I am.
In a catastrophe of historic proportions, Titus, King of Rome, destroyed Jerusalem and expelled the Jewish people from its land, causing me to be born in one of the cities of our exile. But always, it seemed to me that I was born in Jerusalem. In dreams and night visions, I saw myself standing with my Levite brothers in the Temple, as I sang with them the songs of David, King of Israel. It was the merit of Jerusalem that enabled me to write all that God placed in my heart and in my pen.

A page from the Barcelona Haggadah

Fragment of an illuminated Ketuba from the Rivarolo Community, Italy. The Ketuba is illuminated with a picture of the Jerusalem landscape

The building of Jerusalem is a tangible aspect of the Jewish redemption. The following story involving one of the leaders of the Hasidic movement in the eighteenth century demonstrates just how concrete hope for the redemption could be.

When the daughter of Rabbi Levi Yitzhak of Berditchev was to be married, he gave instructions to write in the invitation that the wedding would take place, with God's help, in the holy city of Jerusalem on the first of the month of Tammuz. "And if, God forbid, the Messiah has not arrived by then, the wedding will be held in Berditchev."

(Rabbi H. R. Rabbinowitz, Kosher Humor)

The Temple implements are carried back to the Temple at the top of the hill. By Kafra, the Feldheim Haggadah

Jerusalem of this World and the Heavenly Jerusalem

According to a widely held belief, in addition to the earthly Jerusalem, there exists another -- heavenly -- Jerusalem. In Jerusalem, Heaven and Earth merge; this is the city's uniqueness. According to some opinions, the plural form of the name, Yerushalayim (Hebrew for Jerusalem), shows the dual nature of Jerusalem as a city existing both in Heaven and on Earth.

An expression of the connection between the heavenly and earthly Jerusalems may be found in a popular song about the symbolic figure of the prophet Elijah, who ascended to Heaven in a fiery chariot, but who -- according to tradition -- still walks among us and will be the first to bring news of the redemption.

In Jerusalem there lives
A man by no means young,
Who has built houses throughout the city,
He knows each alley, street, and neighborhood.
He has built Jerusalem for seventy years,
And he dreams that, just as he built the city,
He will lay the cornerstone of the Temple --
On his own hands will he bear it to Elijah the prophet.

Chorus:
He sits patiently and waits for him,
For years he has awaited the moment
Preserving his secret and waiting
When will that day finally arrive?

(From "Al Kapav Yavi," by Yoram Tahar-Lev)

The streets of Jerusalem will be full of children and old people, by Miriam Aranne, Israel

Jerusalem Rebuilt and the Ingathering of the Exiles

In the people's consciousness, the rebuilding of Jerusalem and the city's return to greatness as a beautiful city and center of the Jewish people are closely connected to the end of the exile and the return of the Jewish masses to the land of Israel and Jerusalem.

*Thus says the Lord: I will return unto Zion, and will
dwell in the midst of Jerusalem. . . .
There shall yet sit old men and old women in the streets
of Jerusalem. . . .
And the streets of the city shall be full of boys and girls
playing. . . .
Behold, I will save My people from the east country and
from the west country;
And I will bring them, and they shall dwell in the
midst of Jerusalem. . . .*

(Zechariah 8:3-8)

From the day Jerusalem and the Temple were destroyed the Holy One cannot rejoice, until Jerusalem is rebuilt and He has restored the Jewish people to living there.

(Yalkut Shimoni, Eikhah 1009)

Nothing symbolizes the gathering of the far-flung communities of Israel like the recent return of Ethiopian Jews to the land of Israel and Jerusalem.

The moon stands guard from above
Over a paltry sack of food
The desert under my feet stretches, endless, before me
And my mother promises my little brothers:
Just a little more, a little more,
Lift up your feet --
One last push to Jerusalem

Just a little more, a little more
Soon we will be redeemed
We will not stop walking to the land of Israel
Just a little more, a little more
Lift up your eyes
One last push to Jerusalem

(From "The Journey," Haim Idisis)

Many more passages and sayings concerning Jerusalem express the unity of the Jewish people.

A verse in Psalms (122:3) states: "Jerusalem that is built like a city together." Our Sages explain: "Jerusalem -- a city that joins all Jews **together** in friendship." Jerusalem unites all elements of the Jewish people and symbolizes our unity. The ingathering of the exiles and the gathering of Jews from all countries, even as the city is reconstructed, is the most tangible expression of this unity.

(Jerusalem Talmud, Baba Kama 7:10; Hagigah 3:6)

The vision becomes reality

ᴊerusalem as a Light Unto the Nations

The Makoya (a Japanese sect) dancing in front of the Kotel - the Western Wall

At the end of time, say our prophets and Sages, Jerusalem will be a center not only for the Jewish people; at the end of time, Jerusalem will become a spiritual center and a place for the study of Torah and knowledge for the entire world. Jerusalem will be a "light of the gentiles" (Isaiah 42:6). Members of many nations will come to Jerusalem and be morally influenced to improve their ways:

In various languages, the name "Jerusalem" has become a symbol for the ideal, perfect world -- for the just society. William Blake, the nineteenth century English poet, writes in one of his well known poems that he will not stop struggling with injustice " 'till we have built Jerusalem in England's green and pleasant land."

Scripture and our Sages described the Jerusalem of the future as a spiritual center for all peoples of the world. Even today, not only Jewish students, but students from many different nations come to Jerusalem to acquire knowledge of Jewish traditions, science, and art, with which Jerusalem is replete.

Jerusalem by Reuven Rubin (1958)

*A*nd it shall come to pass in the end of
days, that the mountain of the Lord's house
shall be established at the top of the mountains,
and shall be exalted above the hills; and all
nations shall flow unto it. And many peoples
shall go and say: Come you, let us go up to the
mountain of the Lord to the house of the God of
Jacob; and He will teach us His ways and we
will walk in His paths. For out of Zion shall go
forth teaching and the word of the Lord from
Jerusalem. (Isaiah 2:2-3)

142